TIME, SCIENCE

AND PHILOSOPHY

HECTOR C. PARR

Lutterworth Press
Cambridge

The Lutterworth Press
P.O. Box 60
Cambridge
CB1 2NT

British Library Cataloguing in Publication Data:
A catalogue record is available from the British Library.

ISBN 0 7188 2964 6

Printed in Great Britain by
Hillman Printers (Frome) Ltd.

CONTENTS

PREFACE

All thinking people must ask themselves many questions to which they cannot find the answers. If a question is *empirical*, you would expect to find the answer by your own observation or by consulting an encyclopaedia. If it is *formal*, you should be able to work out the answer yourself, provided you have sufficient skill in logic or mathematics. Questions which fall into neither of these categories often belong to the realm of philosophy, and when you ask what answers philosophers themselves can offer, you frequently find them unable to agree on plausible solutions. What is the universe for? How was it created? Is man just a complex machine, or does the possession of a mind render him fundamentally different from every non-living structure? What exactly is meant by good and evil, justice and injustice, beauty and ugliness? Moreover, are these abstract concepts universal, so that any other conscious beings living in distant parts of the universe will necessarily agree with us in our assessment of them?

This little book maintains that one question above all must be resolved if these mysteries are to be penetrated: the question of the true nature of Time. Our lives are dominated by time; how often during a typical day do we look at the clock or consult a calendar, how often must we hurry because there seems insufficient time for the task in hand, and how often do we wish time moved more slowly, so that the passing minutes, days and years of our life would leave us more room for leisure? Many writers have drawn attention to the strange fact that this passage of time, this concept of a present moment which moves steadily forwards, might be no more than an illusion, a figment of the human imagination with no counterpart in the outside world. Yet most of these authors hesitate to accept the conclusion to which their argument leads, and fail to acknowledge the implications of their own teaching in the rest of their thinking or writing. Taking up the challenge, and trying to view the world without the distorting spectacles imposed on us by this false notion of time, can give a clearer insight into many of the traditional problems of philosophy, and leads to a belief that some of these problems are themselves illusory, in that they evaporate, as it were, when analysed from this new viewpoint. The following chapters suggest that the *mathematician's* concept of time comes closest to its true nature; but the non-mathematical reader need not fear any detailed mathematical knowledge will be needed to follow them. Likewise, although several recent developments in physics and astronomy are relevant to our enquiry, most of the book is written for those with little knowledge in such fields. Chapter Eight discusses some of these developments more fully in order to assess the philosophical theories which have been advanced in recent years, not by philosophers, but by scientists working in the field of sub-atomic physics, as they try to make sense of their remarkable discoveries. Therefore, parts of Chapter Eight may prove slightly perplexing to the unscientific reader, but this chapter can be omitted without the gist of the book's main argument being lost.

Among the questions which the book tries to resolve are the nature of causation and the meaning of free will; it also suggests a way of understanding consciousness, and offers a dispassionate explanation of our belief that human behaviour can be morally right or wrong. The reader will find many other familiar philosophical topics missing; I maintain that the development of mankind is *not* the most important phenomenon in creation, nor is the study of human behaviour and thought the best way to seek an understanding of the universe as a whole.

A few of philosophy's problems are approached from a new direction which might appeal to those whose chief interest lies in this field. The book offers a different view of the current problems in quantum mechanics which may interest some physicists. But it is directed chiefly towards the general reader; none of its arguments are difficult to follow, and if the reader is encouraged to contemplate anew some of the questions he or she has asked unsuccessfully in the past, then the book is serving its purpose.

I am grateful to my old friend Eric Allit for his help and encouragement as the book was prepared for publication.

Hector C. Parr
1997

Chapter 1

PHILOSOPHY AND SCIENCE

INTRODUCTION

Has the universe a purpose, or is its development random and unplanned? What is the human mind, and how is it related to the body and to the rest of creation? Indeed, *is* there anything else in creation other than ideas in the mind? Is man's will truly free, making him master of his own behaviour? What is meant when we judge a certain course of action to be virtuous and on what criteria should we base such a judgement? These are some of the problems philosophers discuss today. Is it not remarkable that very similar questions were being asked by Plato and Aristotle four hundred years before Christ? More than twenty centuries of philosophical thought and argument seem to have brought us no nearer their solutions.

Of course, many of the problems which puzzled the Ancients have now been solved. We no longer ask whether the earth is flat or why the sun rises and sets; we know what causes the rainbow and how far away are the stars. Some progress has been made in understanding even the workings of the human mind and the secrets of life itself. Philosophers cannot claim all the credit for resolving these questions; each has now been taken over by science, and our understanding of them has been advanced by applying the scientific methods of hypothesis and experiment. Perhaps scientists will claim that these successes show the superiority of their methods over those of the philosophers, but the scientists' approach may well be less successful if directed now towards the philosophers' still unsolved problems. The philosopher will claim that questions of ultimate reality, of purpose, of truth or ethics are not only less precise, but also more difficult than any which science has conquered so far. Science has failed to tackle them, not just because it has been too busy, but because its methods are inappropriate and inadequate.

It will be unfortunate, however, if we can respond to these intractable problems only by reiterating their difficulty. We must ask whether they have indeed been approached in the best way, or whether perhaps there are faults in the questions themselves. Are they less meaningful than they appear, or have they been posed in a form that makes solution difficult or impossible? Are there fundamental flaws in the working of the human mind when considering such abstract concepts? The next few pages will suggest four factors that may have hindered the search for philosophical truth over the centuries, and the remainder of the book is a humble exploration of an approach which tries to avoid some of the obstacles encountered in the past.

SCIENTIFIC EVIDENCE

The growth of scientific learning and understanding during the last four hundred years has been quite astonishing, but throughout this period many non-scientists have shown an antipathy towards scientific knowledge, and a reluctance to take it into account in their thinking. As a result many ordinary people, as well as some philosophers and church leaders, have long retained old beliefs which scientific discovery has shown to be untenable. Not untypical was the treatment meted out to Nicolaus Copernicus (1473-1543) after he published his masterpiece *De Revolutionibus Orbium Coelestium*, which advances the hypothesis that the earth, rather than being at the centre of all things, is merely one of the planets, turning on its axis each day and revolving around the sun each year. The teaching of this great book was denounced by both the Roman and Lutheran churches because it seemed incompatible with a belief in man's supreme importance in the universal scheme; indeed it was proscribed in the *Index Librorum Prohibitorum* from 1616 until 1835.

Fortunately none of today's philosophers or church elders show such a degree of bigotry as this, and many are now anxious to study and take on board the results of scientific research when formulating their own doctrines, but their task is far more difficult than it would have been in past years. The body of scientific knowledge has become so vast that no one person can understand in depth more than a small area; yet if we wish to speak with authority on any of philosophy's problems we must strive to acquire a working understanding of what science has to say on the surrounding topics, even if that understanding is necessarily superficial. The author C. P. Snow (1905-1980) claimed that a failure to understand the Second Law of Thermodynamics was as great an educational deficiency as not having read a word of Shakespeare. The teachings of Thermodynamics may seem far removed from considerations of human behaviour or freedom of will, but it is hoped that the following chapters, particularly Chapter Three, will show otherwise (and an attempt is made to explain the Second Law in that chapter). There is a formidable list of other branches of scientific knowledge which impinge to a greater or lesser extent on our personal beliefs. Not only philosophers, but all who claim to hold rational convictions, should have some familiarity with recent research into the structure of matter, the theory of relativity, modern astronomical research and cosmology, the strange and indeterminate world of quantum mechanics, and the remarkable rationalisation of living processes revealed by molecular biology.

ANTHROPOCENTRIC ARGUMENT

The second factor we suggest may have contributed to the slow progress of philosophical thought is that too much importance has often been ascribed to mankind and to life on earth in general, and not enough to the rest of creation. In the days before Copernicus it was understandable that man should believe the earth to be the centre of the universe, created specifically for him

11

to inhabit and furnished to make him comfortable. However, since the sixteenth century our increasing knowledge of the cosmos has pushed the earth ever further into a position of insignificance. A degree of arrogance is a universal component of human nature, and this expresses itself not only in the inflated belief of many individuals in their own importance, but also of organisations and mankind itself, making acceptance of the Copernican doctrine distasteful. An irrational belief that living things are the most important objects in the universe is noticeable even among some scientists, despite their avowed impartiality, as we try to show in Chapter Two.

The study of philosophy often begins with an analysis of human *knowledge*. Since philosophy is a branch of knowledge this might appear to be a good starting point; but if the study scarcely moves away from the human mind to consider the wider issues of the universe at large, it would do better to ignore the narrow field of human learning and start at once with a consideration of the outside world. A book on carpentry may begin with a chapter on the care of tools, but it will serve its purpose badly unless it devotes many more pages to their use, the choice of timber, the different kinds of joint, and woodworking practice in general. The philosophers of the eighteenth century were particularly concerned with knowledge. They considered in depth the difference between *empirical* knowledge, which is derived from experience (including, of course, second-hand experience such as other people's testimony), and *analytic* knowledge, of facts which are self-evident because it would be irrational to believe them otherwise. To illustrate the restricting influence of such an approach, consider how these philosophers attempted to resolve the age-old problem of causality—the relationship that exists between cause and effect—and why we believe that every effect must have a cause. In earlier centuries it had been generally believed that our knowledge of this relationship was *analytic*, that the cause was *logically* responsible for the effect. David Hume (1711-1776) did not accept this doctrine and maintained that our understanding of the relationship must be wholly empirical, resulting only from our observations of actual causes and effects. But surely this argument did not add significantly to our understanding of the problem. The simplest manifestation of causation in action is provided when a small number of independent objects react together under the influence of simple forces, as do the major bodies in the solar system. Newton published his *Principia Mathematica* in 1687, describing in detail how the movements of these bodies are caused by their mutual interaction and the universal law of gravitation. Would it not have been more profitable if the philosophers of the day had taken account of some such real system in their investigation of causation, rather than seeking the solution by a study of human knowledge?

Another undesirable result of this anthropocentric approach is the influence human language has had on the conclusions reached by some thinkers. Language is a tool for communicating our thoughts to others, but being totally man-made it ought to play no more part in the formulation of philosophical doctrine than the type of pen used to write it down. Many examples can be quoted of thinking that has reached confused or erroneous conclusions through being conducted linguistically. It has even been suggested that language is the only factor distinguishing man's reasoning ability from that of animals, our superior intelligence being nothing more than a capacity to use words for thinking as well as for communication. This suggestion cannot be true; no amount of linguistic manipulation will enable an engineer to visualise the forces in the structure of a bridge or a composer to create a symphony. On the other hand there are some whose thinking is necessarily verbal; only by manipulating words in his mind can a poet or playwright create works of merit in his own particular field. There is, however, much middle ground between the types of thinking required of engineers and poets, and human reasoning and creativity can often be accomplished either with or without the use of words. People differ widely in the extent to which they use linguistic methods in their everyday lives. One person can tie a knot by visualising the shape he is creating while another may quietly mouth the words, 'Left over right, right over left'. One motorist may be able to gauge accurately the distance his vehicle would require to stop in an emergency and so will reduce speed as necessary when visibility is poor, while another may need to say to himself, 'It is foggy, so I must drive slowly'. We are all liable to fall into the trap from time to time of confusing a word with the concept it represents, so rendering our reasoning suspect or our message unclear. This is particularly noticeable, and reprehensible, in the world of teaching. A teacher can easily instil into his pupils verbal formulae which they will reiterate whenever suitably prompted, and the teacher may then believe that concepts have been learned or principles understood when in fact the learning is purely verbal. Pupils may be taught to recite in geographical order the rivers of Yorkshire, or to decline irregular verbs, and yet not know where Yorkshire is on a map, nor when to use the first, second or third person of a verb. Some religious practices also involve the repetition of verbal formulae, often with great frequency, requiring less devotion to their meaning than to the regularity of their recitation.

We should not be surprised, therefore, that throughout the ages philosophical discussion has sometimes been no more than disagreement over the meaning of words, though the participants have believed they were resolving questions of universal truth. A lecturer might ask his class, 'What is meant by justice?' thinking that, however difficult his students find it to answer comprehensively, at least they should all understand the question. But whereas half of them may try to give a dictionary definition of the seven-letter word JUSTICE, the other half may take it as read that he and they both understand the word, and that they are required to answer the moral question of how to determine whether justice has been achieved in particular cases. The first group would assume the question referred to the *word* 'justice', and the second group to the *concept* 'justice'.

Much philosophical argument has centred around questions of reality or existence. Of course many questions of this sort are meaningful; it is reasonable to ask whether there exist species of insect with four legs, or planets outside the orbit of Pluto, and these questions may someday be answered, but how should we view solemn discussions on the reality of colour, numbers, or the past? No pronouncement on the existence of these things tells us anything about them we did not know already; if two philosophers disagree here it can only be because they define their terms differently, or assign different meanings to the word 'exist'. Some twentieth-century philosophy has been unduly concerned with the nature and function of language, and is distracted thereby from considering more important and universal matters. The doctrine of the Logical Positivists deals largely with the relationship between language and truth. It tells us that no meaningful statements can be made concerning metaphysical concepts such as *virtue* or *beauty*. Many observers assume that, in discussing this doctrine, they are trying to tell us something about these concepts themselves, whereas in fact they are commenting only on the limitations of the language in which such statements must be framed. Whether or not we can discuss metaphysical topics meaningfully is a different question from whether the concepts themselves are significant. The confusion in many people's minds between ideas and their verbal description runs deeply indeed.

EVIDENCE OF THE SENSES

As a young child gradually becomes aware of its surroundings, it imagines that these surroundings are perceived *immediately*, and that they impinge directly upon its consciousness. We all learn eventually that the relationship is actually indirect, and is made only through the medium of our five senses; we discover that the world disappears if we cover our eyes, and that it sounds less distinct if we stop our ears. Nevertheless, many people must go through life giving little thought to the channels by which they are aware of the outside world, until perhaps in later life failing powers make them realise their total dependence on the senses. Philosophers, to their credit, have considered from earliest times some of the implications of this indirect relationship. Plato, in a well-known passage from the *Republic*, compares our perception of the world to that of prisoners constrained so that they can see only shadows on a wall. They therefore believe that the shadows constitute reality, unaware of the real objects which cast them. Our knowledge of the world outside ourselves is second-hand, and our attempts to understand the true nature of reality must rely to some extent on surmise and on our powers of deduction, for reality does not present itself directly to our consciousness as it may appear to the unthinking.

For many who *have* faced up to this problem, however, distrust of the evidence presented by our senses has been carried too far, and this distrust is another of the factors which has bedevilled much philosophical thinking in the past. Indeed some have been led by these considerations to deny the very existence of the material world which we perceive. This extreme form of idealism, a belief that only 'mind' is real, and that matter and substance are illusions, would probably never have been considered but for the fact that in sleep we have dreams which at the time appear real, but which we later discover to be wholly in the mind. What reason have we to believe the world we observe during the day to be any more real than that which we encounter at night in our dreams? The answer surely lies in the remarkable consistency of the world our senses present to us in the waking state. The tree we saw outside our window yesterday looks almost the same today and will be little different tomorrow. We hear with our ears its howling as the wind passes those same branches we see with our eyes, and if we go outside and bump into it, we shall feel the presence of the trunk in just the same position that we see it. However, is not an even stronger argument than this provided by modern science's description of the reasons lying behind the development of our five senses over the millions of years during which they evolved? They have been refined by natural selection to give an increasingly accurate picture of the external world, the world to which we must constantly react if we are to survive. There is no reason to doubt that the senses give us a good representation of our environment; if they did not, we should not have learnt to conquer it so successfully. Of course we can describe 'reality' at different levels. Our usual view of the tree will show it to consist of trunk, branches and leaves; a magnifying glass would give a different view of the leaves, while a botanist or a chemist may well have diverging conceptions of their structure. But these are just alternative pictures of the same reality, pictures which differ in their degree of detail. The fact that such diverse descriptions can be correlated into the wider concept of a tree without any contradictions is another example of that same consistency which validates the evidence of our senses. An assertion that the tree is no more than an idea in the minds of those who think they observe it leaves a great deal unexplained. It is much simpler to believe that we see it because it is there.

EVIDENCE OF INTROSPECTION

In forming a picture of the external world, the evidence of our own perception is largely to be trusted, but the same cannot be said in relation to the workings of our own minds. Indeed it seems that the nearer we come to the seat of our own consciousness, the less reliable are the results of introspection, and the less plausible and consistent are the impressions we form of what is really there. This is the fourth suggestion we make in our attempt to explain why philosophical argument has so often been inconclusive. We must look into our own minds to discover the true nature of knowledge, the meaning of aesthetic judgement and appreciation, the sense in which we possess free will, or the significance of consciousness itself, and as we do so, nature seems almost contrived to give us the wrong answers.

Nowhere is this more true than when we try by introspection to discover the nature of *time*, and herein is one of the main themes of the present book; the investigation of time in Chapter Three leads to surprising conclusions, and we hope to show in the later chapters that taking these conclusions into our thinking can throw new light on some of the age-old questions of philosophy.

SUMMARY

Four factors suggest themselves when we try to explain philosophy's limited progress in answering the fundamental questions it has considered over the centuries.

(i)   Thinkers have often lacked sufficient scientific knowledge in fields relevant to their enquiries.

(ii)   There is a common tendency to overrate the importance of mankind and the human mind in relation to the overall scheme of the universe; one aspect of this is seen when language is allowed to influence the search for truth, or becomes inadvertently the area being searched.

(iii)   A realisation that we depend wholly on the five senses for our empirical knowledge of the world has often led to an exaggerated distrust of the evidence they present. We should be ready to accept the impressions our senses give of the outside world unless there is strong reason to doubt them.

(iv) However, we should *not* readily accept our first impressions of how the mind works. In particular we must analyse carefully our experience of the passage of time. This can make possible a new approach which simplifies many of the questions we ask, and causes others to vanish when we realise they are really without meaning.

Chapter 2

MAN'S PLACE IN THE UNIVERSE

ASTRONOMICAL NUMBERS

Everyone knows that the universe is big; we often use the adjective 'astronomical' to describe quantities which are much larger than those we normally handle in everyday life, and many of the numbers with which astronomers deal are indeed enormous. This is true whether they refer to the actual *numbers* of astronomical bodies, to their *sizes*, their *distances* or their *ages*, for all these quantities may be far beyond what we can picture adequately. Nonetheless, if we are to have a true conception of man's relationship to the universe, we must make some effort to understand the scale on which it is built, even though we know that effort will be only partially successful.

Most people today can picture the earth as a whole, and many have circumnavigated the globe at some time in their lives. We still think of the earth as large—an impression that is reinforced when we remember the speed of modern aircraft and the fact that they need more than a day to fly around the equator—but the size is not beyond our imagination. The distance of the moon from the earth, about a quarter of a million miles or thirty times the earth's diameter, can also be pictured, and we know men have made the journey there and back. The distance of the sun from the earth, ninety-three million miles, is more difficult to visualise; it is helpful to think not in terms of the speed of an aircraft but rather that of light and radio waves. A radio signal can travel once around the earth in about one seventh of a second; it can reach the moon in about one and a half seconds, but requires eight minutes to reach the sun. Pluto, the most remote planet in the solar system, is many times as far from the sun as we are, so that light or radio waves take over five hours to travel there from the sun.

When we move outside the solar system, distances become quite unimaginable. The nearest star is at a distance of four light-years; a radio signal would take four years to reach it. The distance is so great that if we could visit that star our own sun would itself look just like another star. This fact—that the sun is no more than a typical star, and would appear insignificant from interstellar distances—is just the first step in our attempt to demonstrate the unimportance of the solar system within the universe as a whole. Some of the stars we can see with the naked eye or with a small telescope are many times further away than the nearest; their light may have taken thousands of years to reach us, and light, remember, would travel seven times around the earth in a second.

It might be argued that these distances are not in themselves a cause for wonder. Distances are relative, and saying that the distances of the stars are great is the same thing as saying those we measure on earth are small. But this cannot be said about numbers, which are *not* relative. The number of stars which can be seen from earth without optical assistance is only about six thousand, but a modest telescope can increase this to several million, and many thousands of millions are visible with a larger instrument. These numbers are absolute, and not relative to anything. It is helpful to think of them in relation to the population of the earth, which is about five thousand million; the number of stars readily visible in a good telescope is at least twenty times as great as the number of human beings on the earth.

This surely poses a serious threat to the arguments of those who believe the universe exists primarily to provide a home for mankind. Some may believe that among the stars there are planets like the earth supporting life, and this will be discussed later in the chapter, but maintaining that life has a significant place in the meaning of the cosmos is difficult when we remember how small a part of space it can occupy. Moreover our existence has no effect whatever on the thousands of millions of stars which we observe.

This is only the beginning of the story. One of the most astonishing scientific events of the twentieth century was the discovery that the system described in the last paragraphs, comprising about one hundred thousand million stars, is only one of many. In fact, by coincidence, the number of such systems which modern astronomy can detect is itself about one hundred thousand million, each comparable to our own system and containing a similar number of stars. The distances between these remote systems, or 'galaxies' as they are called, are also beyond imagination. One of the nearest is the Andromeda Nebula, which can be seen with the naked eye on a dark night, and its distance is over two million light-years. When we view it, the light which enters our eyes has been travelling through space since long before the first men appeared on earth, and this is one of the closest galaxies; the furthest which are observable with large telescopes are several thousand times as far away, and their light has travelled towards us for thousands of millions of years. We see the most distant as they existed before the sun and the solar system came into existence.

STRUCTURE OF THE UNIVERSE

A further remarkable discovery was made in the 1920s when Edwin Hubble systematically measured the speeds at which some of these galaxies were travelling. He found that almost all are moving away from us, and the further away a galaxy is the faster it moves. At first sight this seems to imply that we are at the centre of the universe—perhaps mankind after all has some special significance, if only because everything else in space is moving away from him!—but on reflection you will see that this is not the case. Because the rate of recession is proportional to the distance, we would observe the same in whichever galaxy we happened to live. The galaxies are all moving away from each other, and not from some fixed point in space.

This is an appropriate place to consider a problem that troubles many people, and not only those who make a study of philosophy or cosmology. Does space go on for ever, or has it an end? Both alternatives seem problematical; the idea of an infinite space is difficult to comprehend, but if the universe is finite what would we observe as we approached its boundary? A different question is whether the number of *objects* in the universe is finite; if space is finite then so must be the number of stars, but in an infinite space the number of stars might also be infinite, or alternatively there could still be only a finite number, occupying just a finite part of the infinite space available.

A possible way of resolving this question was offered by mathematicians in the nineteenth century, who showed that a space with a finite volume does not necessarily have a boundary. Space is three dimensional; by this we mean that three numbers are required to specify one point in space; a point in a room can be fixed by quoting its distance from the floor and from two adjoining walls; a helicopter's position can be defined by giving its latitude, longitude and height above sea level, or alternatively by giving its distances from three fixed points on the ground. In every case *three* numbers are required; if only one or two are given the position is not fixed, and if four are given then one of these is redundant, and can be calculated from the other three. To take a very simple case, if you quote the distance of a point in a room from the floor, the ceiling, and two adjoining walls, then the distance from the ceiling is unnecessary because you can calculate it when you know the distance from the floor.

No-one can say why our universe is three-dimensional, but we can imagine it otherwise. A two-dimensional space is a *surface*, and one can picture a race of creatures with zero thickness living on the surface of a large sheet of paper. Such beings would specify positions by giving *two* numbers, and would be unaware of the limitations of their universe and unable to visualise three-dimensional space. But it is interesting to reflect that these creatures would be able to live on the surface of a large sphere. They could discover this was indeed the case by circumnavigating their universe and finding themselves, after travelling for a great distance in what they thought was a straight line, back where they started. Even without making such a long journey, they might suspect that space had strange properties if they made geometrical measurements extending over a significant part of their world, because the formulae we all learned at school for the angle sum of a triangle or the circumference of a circle are not quite accurate on the surface of a sphere. *We* can see why, as we observe their world from three-dimensional space, but they would have no such picture, and would be perplexed. They also might ask whether their space is infinite, just as we do about ours, and if they decide it is finite they will wonder what lies beyond its boundaries. But we can see that their space is finite and yet has no boundary. Now just as these two-dimensional beings are unable to picture a three-dimensional space, so we are unable to visualise one that is four-dimensional; but arguing by analogy we can imagine its existence. If our three-dimensional space is *curved* into a fourth dimension in a similar way to that in which the two-dimensional surface of a sphere curves into a third dimension then we too can live in a universe which has a finite volume, but has no boundary. In such a space we can imagine travelling in a straight line and eventually finding ourselves back where we started. So a finite unbounded universe is a possibility. While there is no simple observation astronomers can make to decide the question one way or the other, there are indirect ways in which it should be possible to settle the matter when enough data is available, though the required measurements are difficult and delicate. At the time of writing there is insufficient evidence to decide conclusively whether our universe is finite or infinite.

HISTORY OF THE UNIVERSE

To return now to the main argument, what conclusions can we draw from the expansion of the universe and the resulting recession of the galaxies? The further away a galaxy is situated the greater is its speed of recession, and in the case of those most distant, whose light has taken thousands of millions of years to reach us, the speed becomes a significant fraction of the velocity of light. So what does this imply about the past? Clearly the galaxies must have been closer together in the past, and almost all scientists now believe that the cosmos came into existence in a 'big bang', an immense explosion that began at a single point, generating all the matter and energy in the universe as an expanding fireball. We can measure the speeds of recession of the galaxies with considerable accuracy, and for many we know their distances also, so it should not be difficult to calculate how long ago the big bang occurred. The mathematics is rather complicated because the recession has been slowing down, and there is not yet agreement on the rate of deceleration, but it seems certain that some ten to twenty thousand million years have elapsed since the universe came into being. The ages of the sun and the earth are known to be four or five thousand million years, so these figures are not inconsistent.

Two questions immediately present themselves: (i) what existed before the big bang, and (ii) what caused the big bang? You probably expect the answer, 'we do not know', which would leave you rather dissatisfied but free to formulate your own theories and beliefs. In fact the answer we offer is that both these questions are meaningless. As understood by most cosmologists today, the big bang represented not only the beginning of all the matter and energy in the universe, but also of space and time themselves. Just as the expansion of the universe should be thought of not as the movement of the galaxies into what was previously empty space, but rather as the expansion of space itself—which immediately after the big bang was very small, with matter and energy extremely hot and dense—so also did time itself come into existence at that moment. Asking what preceded it or what caused it is nonsense. This argument must be stressed, for while it is not difficult to explain, it *is* difficult to absorb into one's thinking and one's beliefs.

We can easily understand why the expansion is slowing down. If you throw a ball upwards, it loses speed until it reaches its highest point and then begins to move downwards with increasing speed, returning eventually to the point of projection. The same happens to a rocket which is rapidly accelerated to its maximum speed and then allowed to move freely. Provided this maximum is less than seven miles a second, the earth's gravitational field slows the rocket until it stops and begins to move downwards again. However, if the speed reached is more than seven miles a second the rocket never stops and never returns to earth; the force of gravity becomes less as we move away from the earth, and although the rocket constantly loses speed, the steadily weakening force of gravity is never sufficient to bring it to rest and start it on its return journey. Something very similar happens to the whole universe, for all the bodies in it attract each other gravitationally, and their speeds of recession are constantly being reduced. A mathematician can calculate whether the recession is rapid enough to ensure it will continue for ever, like a rocket starting out from the earth with a greater speed than the critical value, or whether the recession will eventually be stopped so that all the material in the universe will begin to fall back on itself, like a rocket starting with a speed less than the critical value. In this latter case the universe will finally vanish in one devastating implosion which has come to be known as the 'big crunch'. Perhaps it should be mentioned that even if we do find a big crunch is inevitable, there is no immediate cause for concern; space is still expanding and so is certainly less than half-way through its lifetime; it has already existed for more than ten thousand million years, and so will continue for at least as long into the future.

But which of these two possibilities will come about? In order to do the necessary calculation we need to know the average density of matter and energy in the universe as a whole, and at the present time there is much discussion and no agreement on whether this density is above or below that needed to halt the expansion. If we base our figure on the number of stars and the amount of other visible matter, the density is only about one hundredth of the critical value. Observation of the motions of individual galaxies indicates that there must indeed be much more material in each of them than we can actually see, perhaps ten times as much. This still indicates an average density one tenth the critical value, and a universe which will continue expanding for ever. However, we are discussing an area of great uncertainty; more contributions to this all-important average density are constantly being suggested or discovered, and many experts believe that its value may well be greater than the critical value, so sentencing the cosmos to eventual collapse and the end of everything, including space and time themselves, in a colossal catastrophe much like a time-reversal of the big bang. Those who are depressed by this prediction can imagine that the big crunch will be followed by another big bang and the emergence of another universe, which may or may not be like the one we inhabit at present, but there is no justification for such a belief except the wishful thinking of those who do not like to see a good thing wasted.

OTHER WORLDS

In contrast to our uncertainty about the future of the universe, our knowledge of its past history is remarkably complete. Scientists discuss with conviction the conditions which prevailed just a fraction of a second after the big bang, and they can tell you the average temperature and the forces at work during each era of the universe's history. For the first few hundred thousand years the temperature steadily declined but the intensity of the radiation prevented the formation of the chemical elements with which we are familiar. Then after some three hundred thousand years, matter and radiation finally 'decoupled', and the foundations were laid of the universe as we know it. Most of the matter at that time was in the form of hydrogen and helium which began to condense by gravitational attraction to form a first generation of stars and galaxies. Most of the radiation was in the infra-red region, like that generated by a radiant electric fire, and much of this is still travelling through space; but because of the expansion that has taken place during the thousands of millions of years since it was emitted, it is now in the form of radio waves rather than heat, and can be detected easily with today's radio telescopes. The discovery of this 'microwave background radiation' in 1965 provided powerful confirmation of the big bang theory.

Also well understood is the way in which the sun and stars generate their heat by means of a nuclear reaction which converts hydrogen into helium in much the same way as a hydrogen bomb. The history of different types of star can now be described in detail; many end their lives in a spectacular explosion, which we can observe as a 'super-nova', before collapsing into a small body of very high density. At one time we could not understand the source of the heavy elements such as carbon and oxygen which go to make up bodies like the earth, for only hydrogen and helium came into existence as a result of the big bang, but we now know that these super-nova explosions scatter abroad large quantities of all the stable elements. The earth could come into being only after the first generation of short-lived stars had run their course and scattered their debris into space, ready to condense into a second generation of stars. Our sun was formed in this way, with the planets representing some remnants of dust left over when the sun condensed.

We now have detailed knowledge of all the major planetary and satellite bodies in the solar system as well as the length of their days and of their years, the composition of their atmospheres and the range of temperatures on their surfaces. In contrast to this we know very little about planetary bodies orbiting any star other than the sun. It is sobering to realise that even the nearest stars (excluding the sun, of course) are so distant that our most powerful instruments can barely detect the presence of any bodies like the earth in their vicinity. However, there is no reason to suppose that planetary systems are rare; although we do not understand fully how the planets formed, it seems likely that a high proportion of the stars will have planetary bodies moving around them. This means that the number of such planets in our own galaxy may be in the tens or hundreds of thousands of millions, and the number in the cosmos as a whole quite beyond comprehension.

The question that immediately comes to mind concerns the suitability of these bodies for supporting life, and in particular, intelligent life. The earth is remarkably well suited. We have a stable and long-lived source of light and heat in the sun, at just the right distance to provide the temperatures in which life can flourish—high enough to permit life's chemical processes, but not so high as to vaporise water, which seems to be essential in its liquid state. We have an atmosphere of suitable composition and density, a force of gravity sufficient to retain this atmosphere but not so powerful as to limit severely the movement of mobile organisms, and the ready availability on the surface of all the chemical elements which seem to be necessary for life. One's first reaction is to rejoice in our good fortune, but of course this is viewing the situation from the wrong position. Even if there is only one planet in the whole universe capable of supporting life then it is the earth; we *are* a form of life. This observation is an example of a simple but important principle which scientists have graced with the title 'The Anthropic Principle'. This states in effect that our own existence selects in a highly specialised way the environment in which we live. Whether or not the earth is typical of planetary bodies in the universe as a whole, its suitability for life should not surprise us; if it were not so we would not be here.

ALIENS

When we consider the possibility of life existing elsewhere, how common it might be, and whether the emergence of intelligence is likely wherever life has evolved for a sufficient time, the anthropic principle again has something to say; if life in general is common but intelligent life rare, then we should not be surprised that it has evolved on earth. We ask questions such as this because we *are* intelligent, and our existence makes the earth untypical.

It is not only scientists who are intensely curious to know whether life exists elsewhere. The popularity of science fiction and of computer games in which humans interact with alien life-forms shows how general is this fascination, and how powerful the longing to discover that we are not alone. A strong desire to make contact with living creatures other than those on earth may be thought merely a harmless manifestation of our gregarious nature, but in a scientist who should relate to the subject of his investigations in a wholly impartial manner, it can be a handicap, as is well illustrated by the history of Martian observation. When in the nineteenth century an Italian astronomer reported that he had observed some channels on Mars, this was promptly mis-translated into English as 'canals'. Before long an elaborate network of straight canals had been mapped by the American astronomer Percival Lowell (1855-1916), and soon afterwards they were seen by many other observers. Changes in colour of the Martian landscape were interpreted as the growing and withering of vegetation, irrigated by water from the seasonal melting of the polar ice-caps through these canals, which had

28

been constructed by a race of intelligent beings desperately trying to survive on a planet running short of water. Only when photographs were taken in the 1960s from orbiting satellites was everyone convinced the canals had been either an optical illusion or the product of over-active imaginations. In 1977 two spacecraft landed on the surface of Mars to take close-up photographs and perform analyses on soil samples in an attempt to find organic chemicals which would show at least that primitive life forms had existed there at one time. It was clear within a day or two that no such organic material was found, but it was several weeks before the project controllers in USA could bring themselves to admit it. They suggested instead that the experiments must have gone wrong, or the results had become garbled during transmission, or the wrong experiments had been done. Such is man's eagerness to find he is not alone in the universe.

At the time of writing, American scientists have just announced that a meteorite, found in Antarctica in 1984 and supposed to have originated on Mars, contains signs of a micro-organism. It is not clear what evidence exists of the meteorite's extra-terrestrial origin, but the story of Martian investigation suggests that we should approach any such announcement with caution. The promise by the President of the USA, as he campaigns for votes in the forthcoming election, that the country will offer all necessary support to NASA in its search for Martian life, does not increase our confidence that future research will be dispassionate.

It has long been recognised that, if any other planets in our own solar system could support life, then Mars was the most likely, but what about other planetary systems? If we are correct in believing that a high proportion of stars have planets of their own (or even if we are not, and the proportion is low), there might be such an enormous number, and such variety in their constitution, temperatures and atmospheres, that some at least will closely resemble the earth. The likelihood of life developing on such planets is discussed in a later chapter; opinions differ, but there is general agreement that, because the numbers are so great, there must be some besides our own on which living material has appeared. Opinions differ even more widely on whether any of these will have evolved intelligence like our own.

Considerable effort and expense is being devoted at the present time in attempts to communicate with any living creatures that may be out there, but the naïvety of some of these experiments is rather amusing. Radio waves provide the most feasible medium by which communication would be established; radio astronomy has been developing now for about fifty years, and recognisable signals are received from many different types of astronomical body. None of these has ever shown evidence of intelligent creation, but there was quite a stir when the first *pulsar* was discovered in 1967; the radio signal from this object was flashing on and off about once a second in a way that no known celestial source could explain; the astronomers who made the discovery flippantly called it LGM1, standing for 'Little Green Men'. Fortunately they were able to keep the information from the news media until they had established that the signals were from a rapidly rotating planetary body, and not from an alien civilisation trying to make galactic friends! At the present time an elaborate and expensive project is in progress whereby the whole sky is being scanned with a network of radio telescopes and an automatic detection system that will call for human intervention only when a signal appears to be of artificial origin. Much thought has been given to the likely form that any signal from intelligent beings will take, and we should have no difficulty distinguishing it from natural phenomena. It would indeed be exciting to have firm evidence of the existence of an alien civilisation outside our own solar system, and the efforts are to be applauded, but what shall we do if such signals are received? We are told that we must establish communication with the creatures sending us these messages, develop a common language, and then try to learn from them not only the secrets of their technological progress but also their social customs. Such beings may well have had a civilised society far longer than we have, and must have solved all the problems which seem to threaten our own, such as warfare, disease and pollution; learning how a more advanced civilisation has dealt with these issues may help us handle them ourselves, and ensure the survival of our race. Sadly, this is nonsense. Those who talk seriously in this way have no understanding of the times and distances involved. Even if there are millions of such civilisations in the cosmos as a whole, they will still be very rare in our own locality, not only because the conditions necessary for life are so stringent, but also because no civilisation can hope to exist forever. If civilisations last on average for a million years, this is still only a fraction of a thousandth of the lifetime of a planet such as the earth, so that even if every star had a planet in orbit on which civilised life appeared, less than one in a thousand would be sustaining such life at any one time. Remembering that the nearest star is four light years distant, even if life is prolific throughout the universe it seems highly unlikely that our nearest civilisation will be within a thousand light years. How can you communicate with anyone when it requires thousands of years to get the answer to a single question, particularly when you start with no common language?

Even more naïve are the efforts being made to send out into space information about our own existence and culture. When Pioneer 10 was launched in 1973, it contained a gold plaque on which was engraved a picture of a man with his hand raised as a sign of peace, a diagram of a hydrogen atom and a plan of the solar system. How can interested aliens ever distinguish this craft from the millions of pieces of rock which move around in space? How could it be stopped and captured? What use is a picture of a man to an alien who is himself in an entirely different form? Later spacecraft have contained video discs, recordings of Bach and a message from the Secretary General of the United Nations. Moreover, in 1973 a radio message was beamed into space for all listening aliens to interpret. It consisted of one thousand, six hundred and seventy nine pulses – and because the number one thousand, six hundred and seventy nine can be factorised in only one way, the recipients would immediately realise that the pulses represent points on a rectangle measuring twenty three by seventy three, revealing a lesson in binary arithmetic, a diagram showing the atoms of the elements essential for life on earth, and a picture of a matchstick man. Highly trained scientists can devise such simplistic projects only because they, like most of us, fervently hope that there are other rational creatures in the universe, and long to make contact with them to relieve the loneliness generated by contemplation of the barren and inhospitable depths of space.

INTER-STELLAR TRAVEL

Even more remote from reality is the belief many have that we could travel to other worlds outside the solar system, or that aliens from these worlds could land on earth. Such beliefs again ignore the times and distances involved, and the laws of physical science, which cannot be broken by living creatures however intelligent they are. If a space craft is to escape the earth's gravity it must be accelerated up to a speed of seven miles per second. To escape the sun's gravity and fly out of the solar system requires twenty six miles per second; part of this speed can be provided by the earth's own velocity in its orbit, but a velocity greater than this is required if the craft is still to be moving at a useful speed after escaping the sun's clutches. With present-day fuels and technology these speeds are at the limit of what we can achieve, but improvements in the next few decades may possibly enable a craft to leave the solar system and still be travelling at about ten miles per second. If it then travels to the nearest star the journey will take no less than seventy four thousand years. It would be difficult to persuade passengers to embark on such a journey, knowing they would surely die before completing one thousandth of it. It may be argued that new sources of power could some day be developed that would permit higher speeds, but the gulf between what is required and what is presently available is so enormous that one can assert with confidence that it will never be bridged. In any case, however highly developed fuel technology becomes, mankind will always have difficulty meeting his own energy requirements here on earth. There will never be a time when the colossal amount of energy required would be made available just to send two or three people on a journey from which they would never return.

It has been suggested by some who understand these distances that whole colonies could be sent out on voyages of galactic exploration. Such a colony could be self supporting, with an ecology based on total recycling of waste, and could travel for unlimited distances and times. Again, this can only be described as absurd; who would be prepared to sacrifice his own life and that of the next two thousand generations of his family so that some distant descendant might possibly find an inhabitable planet? Furthermore, every argument against man travelling outside our own solar system is also a reason forbidding the arrival within it of creatures from another; aliens from outer space will forever remain within the realm of science fiction and computer games.

The number of heavenly bodies is so great that we can easily believe some of them, perhaps millions of them, are supporting simple living organisms. Out of these it seems possible that some will have developed a degree of intelligence. Nevertheless, we must admit, however reluctantly, that the possibility of our ever receiving signals from another civilisation is small, and that of establishing two-way communication with them, or of meeting them here or elsewhere, is nil.

THE SIGNIFICANCE OF LIFE

Perhaps the most fundamental question that can be asked is whether or not the universe is unfolding in accordance with some plan or purpose. If it is, then the emergence of life is surely among the most important parts of that plan. When we contemplate the wonder and richness of life on earth we have difficulty believing it has all developed by chance. The anthropic principle teaches us that we should not be surprised that the surface of the earth is so suitable for the development of life, but the fundamental difference of living creatures from inanimate matter seems to provide compelling evidence that they are not merely the result of some accident. Those who argue this case, however, can do so effectively only if they have taken on board the teachings of modern astronomy. They must admit that the universe is far bigger and more complex than it needs to be to support a few colonies of life like our own here on earth, and the regions in which life is possible are rare indeed. The vast expanses of interstellar space are much too cold, and the stars far too hot. If the purpose of the cosmos is to provide a home for life, a more inefficient and wasteful way of doing so is difficult to imagine.

We shall continue the discussion of purpose versus chance in the final chapter of this book. Perhaps the ideas presented in the intervening chapters will help us to make an informed choice at the end.

Chapter 3

TIME

FAMILIAR EXPERIENCES

The more familiar an experience, the less inclined are we to look for an explanation, or to acknowledge that an explanation is necessary or possible.

To take one example, consider the universal observation that material objects possess weight, and fall down when unsupported. Can you think back to a time in your early childhood when you had not heard of gravitation or Sir Isaac Newton? Did you find it perplexing that anything which slipped out of your hand always moved downwards? Did you ask your parents why your toys all travelled unaided towards the floor? It is most unlikely. The effect of gravity seemed so natural that you would never give it any thought.

Newton did not completely explain gravitation, but he did show that whatever *is* its cause, also explains the movements of the moon and all the bodies in the solar system. Realising that the falling of bodies *needed* an explanation is an even more impressive indication of his genius than the actual 'Theory of Gravitation' he devised. There were probably several mathematicians of his day who could have arrived at the 'Inverse Square Law' from the observed movements of the heavenly bodies; but only Newton had the insight to relate these movements to anything as mundane as the falling of an apple from a tree.

THE NATURE OF TIME

In this chapter we consider some concepts which are even more familiar than that of gravitation, and which consequently have received less consideration from scientists and philosophers than they deserve. These ideas are all concerned with the real nature of *time*.

It is true that some of the difficulties associated with the concept of time have been acknowledged by philosophers of all ages, from Parmenides (515 BC), who argued that all change is impossible, to John McTaggart (1866-1925), who convinced himself that time itself cannot exist. The objections raised by most of these thinkers arose from considering time to consist of a succession of instants, each having no duration; similar objections can be aimed at our conception of distance, leading to such puzzles as the well-known paradox of the race run by Achilles and the tortoise. Achilles gives the animal a start, but by the time he reaches the tortoise's starting point, it has moved a further distance away from him; using this argument repeatedly we can show that Achilles can never overtake the tortoise. All such false reasoning has now been banished by the modern mathematician's idea of a *continuous variable*, and the sound logical basis we now have for our definition of a 'rate of change' and the summing of infinite series.

But time presents several other problems which are perhaps more subtle than these, and which are not so easily disposed of; we shall consider here the three most perplexing of them.

(i)   Why is there one time which we call 'now' or 'the present', such that all other times can be described as either 'before' or 'after' the present?

(ii)   Why does the moment we call 'now' seem constantly to move forward? The idea that time is steadily advancing or flowing is so familiar, or so 'obvious' as we might say, that any suggestion it is an illusion will be met with incredulity or opposition. But later in the chapter we hope to show that the moving of time plays no part in the scientist's description of the world, and that indeed the notion itself involves a contradiction.

(iii)   Why do the two possible directions of time appear so different? Almost all simple processes, such as a stone rolling down a hill, an egg falling onto the floor and breaking, or a flower withering and dying, appear nonsensical if recorded by a cine- or video-camera, and played back in reverse. We know that in the real world broken eggs do not collect themselves together on the floor and jump intact onto the shelf above, and stones do not roll uphill. We must ask, 'Why not?'

The concept of time permeates all our thinking; if there are disparities between time in the real world and assumptions we have been making thoughtlessly about it, this cannot fail to impinge on our beliefs. Our views on questions of causation, purpose and free will are all closely related to our impression of the passage of time. Causation refers to possible influences events can have on the future, never on the past; if we need to change our view of the distinction between past and future we must then reconsider whether the future is determined by the present. Any discussion of free will is likewise about the capacity of thinking beings to influence the future. And the whole idea of *purpose* is dependent on a belief that time is moving onward, and that our actions today can be chosen to bring about particular outcomes in the days that follow.

If, as we are suggesting, philosophers have given insufficient consideration to the nature of time, then any re-appraisal of the concept may well necessitate a major reconsideration of their beliefs. And if we find that some aspects of our view of time are mere illusions, the influence of this on philosophical argument might be great indeed.

THE MATHEMATICIAN'S TIME

Before considering the three questions posed above, let us examine the way time enters into some of the phenomena studied by mathematicians and physicists, and how they illustrate the function of time when they describe such phenomena.

To start with a simple example, consider a walker who leaves home at noon, walks six miles Northwards at 3 m.p.h., stops for an hour to eat his sandwiches and enjoy the view, and then walks

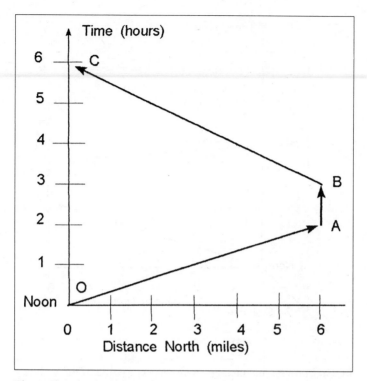

Fig. 1. Showing how the walker's position in one dimension changes with respect to time.

back home at 2 m.p.h. He will arrive home at 6 p.m. This is all well illustrated by Fig. 1, in which *time* is measured vertically and *distance* horizontally. The line OA shows his distance North increasing steadily as time increases from Noon to 2 p.m. Then AB shows that his distance from home does not change during the following hour, and BC that he steadily approaches home again between 3 p.m. and 6 p.m. If our walker were to return home by a different route, then a more complicated model would be required, which we could construct out of cardboard, or illustrate in perspective as in the Fig. 2. Here we measure *distance North* to the right, *distance East* in the direction towards the viewer, and *time* vertically upwards. The reader might like to examine the illustration and try to describe in words the walker's journey. Notice that we represent *Northwards, Eastwards* and *time* by three lines each of which

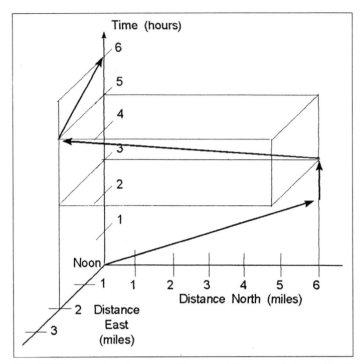

Fig. 2. Showing the changes with respect to time of the walker's
position in two dimensions.

is at right angles to the other two.

If now our walker decides to make a journey in a helicopter,
in which he is free to travel *Northwards, Eastwards* and *upwards*,
it is impossible to construct a model along the same lines as above.
We should then need to draw *four* lines (remembering we need
one for *time*) each of which is at right angles to the other three; as
we live in a three dimensional world these four lines cannot be
drawn. But it is possible to *imagine* the existence of a four
dimensional world in which we could construct such a model.
Although it is not possible actually to see the model in the mind's
eye, or to draw it, we can argue by analogy that it would be
possible if we lived in four dimensions.

Anything which happens at a particular place and at a
particular time, such as a battle, an explosion, or a walker
stopping to take a rest, we shall call an *event*. And if you
succeeded in imagining the model described in the last

paragraph for illustrating the helicopter flight, you should have little difficulty extending the *North, East* and *upward* lines (in both directions) so that they span the whole of space, and the *time* line to include the whole of time, from the creation of the universe to its end. Every event which has ever occurred or will occur in the future will then have its own unique position on your imaginary model.

We cannot construct or draw such a model, but for most purposes it suffices to represent only *two* dimensions of space, and *one* of time, giving an illustration like Fig. 2. On this we were able to show the movement of our walker over a period of time provided he stayed on a two-dimensional surface, such as the land surrounding his home. We can imagine the surface moving upwards (carrying the walker with it) as time progresses; any events which occur at a particular time, such as the simultaneous extinguishing of all the street lights in a town when a power cut occurs, will be represented on our illustration by points which are all in the same horizontal plane.

'NOW'

Let us consider the three questions posed earlier. The first one, asking why we are constantly aware of a 'present' time, is easily answered. Every thought we have is itself an *event*, for it occurs in a particular place (our brain) and at a particular time. It follows from this that every other event in the universe must occur either at an earlier time, a later time, or the same time as that thought; those that take place at the same time are described as 'now'. There is no more mystery about this than there is in the fact that some people's homes are at a higher altitude than ours, some at a lower altitude, and some the same.

(It must be mentioned that Einstein's theory of relativity, in denying the existence of absolute 'simultaneity', throws some confusion over the argument of the previous paragraph. But the practical consequences of this become apparent only when enormous speeds are involved. To rewrite the above paragraph taking full account of relativity would complicate it greatly, but would not invalidate the argument. This will be discussed further in Chapter Eight.)

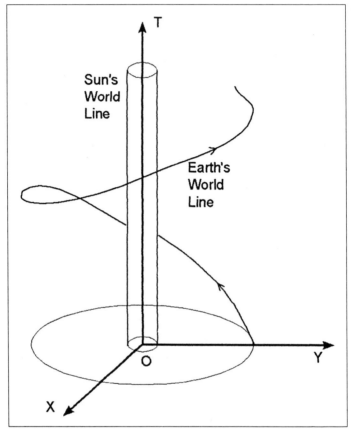

Fig. 3. World Lines of the Sun and Earth.

Now look at Fig. 3. This represents on a space-time diagram the motion of the earth around the sun. Because the earth's orbit lies in a plane we only need two dimensions to represent it. We assume the sun does not move, and draw through it two lines at right angles, OX and OY in the plane of the orbit. We can at any time indicate the position of the earth by quoting the values of x and y, the respective distances of the earth from OY and OX. (Either of these values can be negative if the earth is on the 'wrong' side of the line.) We then draw the line OT at right angles to both OX and OY to represent time.

Because the sun remains at rest the x- and y-values of its centre are always 0. But it has existed for several thousand million years, and is expected to live for at least as long into the future, so its centre must be represented on our diagram not by the point O but by the line OT, extending a great distance in both directions. We call this the 'world-line' of the sun's centre. The whole sun itself will be represented on the x-y plane by a disc (not a sphere, because we can show only two space-dimensions on our diagram), and this becomes a long, straight column as shown, when we take into account its continuous existence as time progresses.

The earth is too small for its size to be shown on the diagram, but because it moves once around the sun each year, its world-line must be a helix, rather like the hand-rail of a spiral staircase.

Each body in the solar system has its own world-line; with patience we could represent them all on a diagram like Fig. 3. In fact every body in the universe, every star, every particle of dust, has its own world-line. And world-lines can react with each other; if two moving billiard balls collide then their world-lines meet and separate again, forming a letter 'X'; if a rock breaks into two its world-line bifurcates like a letter 'Y'. And it is not only when world-lines meet that they can influence one another; the helical form of the earth's world-line owes its shape to the gravitational attraction of the sun; if the sun did not exist the earth's line would be almost straight.

In recent years physicists have made remarkable progress in understanding how different bodies influence each other, on scales ranging from individual parts of an atomic nucleus to the galaxies themselves. Their findings are usually expressed as mathematical equations relating the x, y, z and t values of bodies as they react with one another (where z stands for the third space value which we cannot show, and t stands for time). But in their off-duty moments they must sometimes try to picture these relationships as interactions between the bodies' world-lines, and may even secretly draw x-y-t diagrams in attempts to visualise more clearly the meaning of their equations.

What has now happened to our belief that time is constantly flowing or progressing? Looking again at Fig. 3, we can imagine a horizontal plane at any height we choose above the base-plane

OXY. As time moves on, then this plane will move steadily upward; at any instant the position of the earth is shown by the point where this moving plane is cut by the earth's helical world-line, and we can easily see that this point moves around the sun as indeed it should. But it is an astonishing fact that this progression of time, this moving of the plane representing space in our diagram, plays no part in the physicist's description of the world, or his attempts to understand its working. The fact that there is one particular time called 'now', and that this appears to be constantly advancing, has no effect on his equations; in other words t enters into these equations on very much the same terms as x, y or z. Our impression that the value of t seems always to be changing is quite irrelevant. The picture of the universe which our space-time diagrams give us is no longer a moving picture; it is purely static, different parts of it representing the world as it was, as it is now, and as it will be. Could it be that in the absence of conscious minds there is no movement of time, that the concept is just an illusion, something created within the brain?

It may be objected that in posing this question we are begging another one, namely that of whether or not the future is *determined* in advance. If the whole history of the universe is laid out on a huge space-time diagram, there appears to be no more opportunity for today's happenings to influence the future than they have of influencing the past. The question of free will seems to have been settled in committee without any opportunity for a debate or a free vote. In fact this is not so; there is a fallacy in supposing that to accept this four-dimensional picture is to assume the future is already determined because 'it already exists'. For another way of saying this is, 'it exists at the present time', which is clearly not the case; what exists 'at the present time' is only what is illustrated on one horizontal plane in Fig. 3. Indeed the word 'exists', being in the present tense, necessarily refers only to one horizontal plane in the figure; we ought not to say that the whole space-time 'exists' in the sense the word is normally used. We should not be surprised if our language proves inadequate for describing a picture that was never imagined during the period in which that language was evolving. So questions such as the meaning of *causation* and *free will* are still wide open, and will be discussed in detail in later chapters.

There is a further and possibly stronger argument showing that the 'flow' of time must be an illusion. We say that the time is constantly *changing* as we watch the hands of our watch move, but a consideration of the concept of 'change' reveals a fundamental contradiction. One thing can be said to 'change' only in relation to something else. In everyday speech this 'something else' is usually time itself. If the clothing we are wearing at 2 o'clock differs from that we wore at 1 o'clock, we say we have 'changed' our clothes; if the money we held yesterday in pounds is now in francs, we have 'changed' our money; if the wind this morning blew from the North, but in the afternoon blows from the East, the wind has 'changed'. Mathematicians sometimes use the word in another context in which the second of the two concepts is *not* time, as when they say the circumference of a circle 'changes with the radius'. But in every case *two* things are involved, one of which changes 'with respect to' the other. So what can possibly be meant by saying the time is constantly changing? Changing with respect to what? To time itself? Do we mean that the time now is later than it was previously? Is not this just a tautology? It means no more than saying that Mount Kilimanjaro is higher than all mountains which are not as high as Kilimanjaro. We even talk about the 'speed' of time; time is said to 'go quickly' when we are happy and 'go slowly' when we are not. But how fast does it really go. One minute per minute? The idea of time 'going' or 'moving' can have no meaning; if time appears to 'go quickly' this can only mean that some process in the mind is actually 'going slowly'.

In this way we are driven to the conclusion that the 'flow' or 'passage' of time is a deception. Time is no more than one of the four co-ordinates we must use to specify the location of events in space-time. Admittedly, events can be arranged into temporal order just as they can be placed in spatial order, but there is no counterpart in the real world for the imagined 'now', or for the 'movement' of time.

We cannot yet say we have fully answered question (ii) above, for we have as yet offered no explanation of the strong conviction everyone has that time really *does* move; but we shall leave the problem unresolved until we have considered question (iii) also; perhaps in resolving (iii) we shall throw further light on (ii).

THE ASYMMETRY OF TIME

To gain some insight into problem (iii), the apparent *irreversibility* of time, we consider a number of simple activities, in some of which a time-reversal is clearly ridiculous, and some in which it is not.

Imagine a film being made to illustrate the rotation of the earth, and its movement around the sun. If viewed from above the North Pole, the earth will be seen to rotate anticlockwise once a day, and it will move around the sun anticlockwise in an elliptical orbit, moving slightly faster in the part of the orbit nearer the sun than in the part further from the sun. Now let us run the film backwards. The earth will be seen to rotate *clockwise* once a day, and to move clockwise around the sun in its elliptical orbit, moving slightly faster in the part of the orbit nearer the sun. This representation is clearly wrong — things are moving in the wrong direction, but it is perfectly feasible; the reversed motion is still in accordance with the laws of mechanics and gravitation. The same would apply if the film showed the motions of all the planets in the solar system and included the small influences that each planet has on the movements of all the others. If time were running backwards all these movements would be possible they would merely be in the wrong direction.

But now suppose a film is made to show the effect the sun has on the *temperature* of different points in the earth's atmosphere as the earth turns on its axis. Not surprisingly, that side of the earth which faces the sun, the 'day' side, will be seen to be warmer than the 'night' side on which no sunlight falls. This will still be true if the film is run backwards. But look more carefully. The hottest part of the day is usually not noon, when the sun is still beaming down its light and heat; it is more likely to be about 3 p.m. when the sun has been beating down for a further three hours. Now look at this film in reverse; the earth turns the other way, and the little thermometers give

44

their highest readings at about 9 o'clock in the morning. This does not make sense; it seems that the air heats up because it knows how much longer sunlight will fall on it. A reversal of time in this case produces a situation which is clearly not in accord with our common experience.

If this were all we could say about the situation we would simply accept it as a fact that the laws of physics must themselves be time-asymmetric. We may not be able to explain why this is the case, but there are many features of the fundamental laws of nature which we cannot explain; although enormous progress has been made throughout the twentieth century in theoretical physics, and much that was not understood in the past is now explained with near certainty, more problems have in their turn presented themselves, and it seems unlikely the day will ever come that we understand completely the workings of nature. If some of the laws are not time-reversible, so be it.

But let us look again at this heating by the sun of the earth's atmosphere. The nature of heat is well understood; molecules of a gas move at high speed, and the higher the temperature the greater is the average speed. The movement of each molecule is in a straight line at constant speed until it collides with another or with some solid material, and then the way it rebounds can readily be calculated. And the rules which describe this motion *are all time-reversible*. A film showing the dancing of gas molecules can be run backwards, and they continue to behave impeccably. What about the radiation which flows from the sun? This can be regarded as a vast number of small particles called *photons* all travelling at the speed of light. The laws governing the production of a photon on the hot surface of the sun are well understood, as are the laws governing its absorption by a molecule of gas, liquid or solid material on earth and the consequent increase in that molecule's heat energy. And these laws, like all the fundamental laws of science, also are time-reversible. So we appear to have a strange contradiction here. If we look at the individual molecules of the atmosphere, or the individual photons of light and heat from the sun, then their behaviour *is* time-reversible, but if we take a more general view and look at the same process from a greater distance, as it were, then this is *not* time-reversible.

ENTROPY

To help resolve this paradox, consider an even simpler example. Pour out a cup of hot tea, and it will gradually cool down to room temperature, which will itself have been raised slightly by the heating effect of the tea. When the two temperatures are equal then no further change will occur. This effect is clearly not time-reversible; however long you look at a cup of cold tea it will never decide to draw heat out of its surroundings, thereby heating itself to boiling point, and cooling the surroundings slightly. Heat never flows from a cooler to a hotter body. This is an example of a principle known as the Second Law of Thermodynamics, which was first enunciated by engineers trying to improve the efficiency of steam engines in the nineteenth century, but which has been found subsequently to have implications in many other fields. These engineers derived a formula which, when applied to any collection of objects, gave the value of a quantity they called 'entropy', and they discovered that, if there is no interference from outside, the total entropy of a group of objects never decreases, and usually increases, when they react together in any manner. If we apply this to the example above, as the tea cools it loses both heat energy and entropy, but whereas the surroundings gain exactly the same amount of heat energy as the tea loses, they gain *more* entropy than the tea loses, so that the total entropy of the tea-plus-surroundings increases. The cold tea cannot heat up of its own accord, as this would represent a decrease in the total entropy of the system.

In fact this is not quite true. The total amount of heat energy possessed by the molecules of tea and the surrounding molecules of the air in the room cannot change without outside interference, but there is a random element in the way in which this total is shared out between all the molecules involved. If we start with the tea and its surroundings at the same temperature, then there will in the future be tiny variations of the average temperature of the tea, and hence small changes, upwards and downwards, of the total entropy. But the probability that the tea would ever become measurably hotter than the air around it is so small that we can ignore it totally. The state of affairs in which the two temperatures are so nearly equal that no measurement could distinguish them is by far the most *probable* situation. It is not *impossible* for the tea to reach boiling point again, but it is overwhelmingly *improbable*. The entropy of a system of bodies can be regarded as a measure of its *likelihood*; the constant increase in the entropy of a system represents its progression to a state of affairs which is more and more probable.

The Second Law of Thermodynamics is not time-reversible, but this does not violate the principle stated above that the fundamental laws of physics are time-reversible, for it is not one of the fundamental laws; it is a secondary law describing in general terms the behaviour of large numbers of particles each of which obeys the primary laws, and all of these *are* time-reversible.

We can now see where the asymmetry of time comes from. The most probable natural state of a closed room is the state in which all its contents are at the same temperature. Then there can be no transfer of heat from one body to another, and entropy stays at its maximum possible value, except for the tiny variations caused by the random transfer of small amounts of heat. It then makes no difference which way time is thought to move; the temperature of all objects in the room stays the same. We cannot obtain a hot cup of tea in the room without interfering from outside, either by bringing it in, or introducing a source of heat. This results in an unstable situation which, as it returns to equilibrium, increases the total entropy up to its maximum value. *We* introduced the asymmetry by bringing in the cup of tea; in one time-direction there is no cup of tea in the room; in the other there is a cup of tea at an unstable temperature, and the situation moves towards equilibrium.

When we apply this reasoning on a larger scale, the implications are profound. Everyone knows that the sun is the ultimate source of most of the energy we have here on earth, whether it be energy from coal, oil, falling water or the winds. And energy can flow from the sun only because it is hotter than the earth; if both were at the same temperature we would have no source of energy, little of significance would happen on the earth, and there certainly would be no life.

EFFECTS OF THE UNIVERSAL EXPANSION

The universe is such an interesting place only because of the great differences of temperature between objects like the sun and the stars on one hand, and those like the earth and planets on the other. The question that still requires an answer is, 'what was the interference that introduced this diversity into the universe, that put it in a state of low entropy?' The answer is not difficult to find; the explanation of the low entropy of the universe lies in its *expansion*. The influence of this on the universal thermodynamics is to create and preserve a low entropy situation. Were it not for the expansion then the universe would always have been in a state of maximum entropy; all the contents of space would remain at the same temperature, and the universe would be in a condition of featureless uniformity.

In his book *Space and Time in the Modern Universe* (see Bibliography), Paul Davies (b.1946) gives a physicist's description of how this state of uniformity first came to be broken in the early life of the universe. The movement of particles in the initial 'primordial fireball' following the 'big bang' was totally random and uniform, but because of the expansion, and the rapid lowering of temperature, the process of forming the more stable heavy elements from the hydrogen initially produced was 'turned off' before it had proceeded very far, locking up a vast supply of nuclear energy which could subsequently be released in the centres of the sun and the stars. So at an early stage in its history the universe was in a highly unstable state, a state of low entropy, which fortunately has not yet dissipated.

The expansion is still proceeding, and continues to exert an influence on the contents of space, tending to maintain differences of temperature, and a value of entropy lower than the maximum value. A simple model should show the plausibility of the argument. Imagine a cylinder and piston like those of a steam engine; suppose the cylinder contains air, and also some small solid bodies. If these have not been disturbed for a while then the bodies and the air will be at the same temperature. Now pull the piston outwards to increase the volume occupied by the air; the temperature of the air will immediately fall, but that of the solid material will only gradually follow, for it will take time for heat to be conducted from the inside to the surface where it can be given up to the surrounding air. Pulling out the piston is, of course, an interference from outside, and it has generated an unstable situation, with a temperature difference between the air and the solid material. The cylinder represents the whole of space, the solid bodies represent the stars and other bodies, and the molecules of air represent the photons of radiation which transfer heat and light from body to body. Pulling out the piston increases the volume of air just as the expansion of the universe raises the volume available for these photons, and also reduces their energy. It was explained in the previous chapter how astronomers discovered some years ago that radiation originating from quite an early stage in the life of the universe is still pouring down onto the earth; but whereas it was actually emitted from gases at a temperature of about 3000°C, because of the expansion of the space through which it has been travelling for billions of years, it now looks as if it had come from matter at only about three degrees above absolute zero. The average temperature of the earth is, of course, much higher than this, and that of the sun and stars higher still. (The fact that these larger bodies now have their own nuclear source of energy does not invalidate the argument, but does mean that the temperature differences are greater than they would otherwise be, and they will persist much longer than if they relied solely on the 'thermal inertia' of these bodies.)

When we consider other forms of energy besides heat the concept of entropy is easily extended to encompass them. The most familiar of these is the gravitational energy of bodies which can fall together, such as any pair of astronomical objects, or the earth and a stone on the edge of a cliff; if this falls to the bottom its potential energy changes firstly to energy of motion, and then to heat energy when it strikes the ground. The initial position of the stone represents a low entropy state, and the final situation in which all the energy has become heat represents the maximum possible entropy; this is the most *likely* state, and the possibility of it spontaneously reverting to the initial one, with the stone at the top of the cliff, is remote. The fact that the stars and galaxies in the heavens have not yet fallen into each other as a result of their mutual gravitational attraction is another manifestation of the low entropy of the universe at the present time, and here again its expansion provides an explanation. The speed with which the distant bodies in space are rushing apart means that it will be many billions of years before gravity is eventually able to reverse the process, and start the contraction which will finally give rise to the 'big crunch' described earlier.

In recent years it has been suggested by cosmologists that the initial conditions existing just after the big bang, and on which the present state of the universe depends so critically, must themselves have been highly unlikely, and have not yet been explained. But at the present time these early moments are not understood well enough for any conclusions to be drawn from our ignorance, and we should accept the expansion and initial conditions of the universe as an explanation, as complete as we can hope for with our present knowledge, for the low entropy and the irreversibility of many of the processes we observe. If there were no universal expansion, and if the initial conditions of the universe had not resulted in atomic, chemical and gravitational instability to provide sources of energy, there would be no temperature differences and nothing would happen to distinguish one direction of time from the other.

WHY TIME APPEARS TO FLOW

We can now return to question (ii), and look again at the apparent 'flow' of time. It was suggested by Sir Arthur Eddington (1882-1944) in his book *The Nature of the Physical World* (see Bibliography) that there might be some sort of 'entropy clock' in the brain of a conscious individual. This could explain our belief that time progresses; the gradual increase of entropy within the brain might be sensed as a steady flowing of time from past to future. This would also account for our conviction that the flow of time can occur only in one direction.

But no such hypothetical entropy clock needs to be invented. An essential feature of consciousness is the continual formation within the mind of *memories*. These include not only memories of major events, which may stay with us throughout the rest of

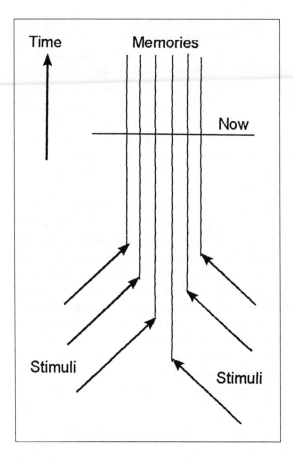

Fig.4. The accumulation of memories in the brain.

our lives, but also those more fleeting memories which last only a few days or a few seconds. Even if we are totally inactive we still have, at each instant of time, a memory of having lived the previous instant; only when we are asleep have we no memories of this sort. The constant inflow of stimuli and creation of memories is represented on a space-time diagram in Fig. 4. Memories, like any other records of events, can only relate to *past* events; this is one of the less obvious results of the Second Law of Thermodynamics, and we discuss it at length in a later chapter. (The reader is asked to take it on trust for the present, but is unlikely to dispute the fact that memories, history books, photographs and sound recordings never present a record of *future* events.) Throughout our waking lives there is a constant inflow of data and a constant formation of memories in the brain, as Fig. 4. illustrates, and herein lies the explanation of our impression that time moves, and can move in only one direction. Some members of the animal kingdom clearly have shorter memories than we have, but if a creature has no memory at all it seems certain it will not experience the movement of time.

How can we be sure our memories are true representations of past events? At each moment of our life we seem to have a record of all previous moments; we appear to be just *visiting* the present, having already visited every past moment. If we have any reason to doubt the accuracy of our memories we can always corroborate them by referring to external records; we can look at our school reports, our collection of photographs or last year's diary. But has it ever occurred to you that we would have exactly the same impressions if these memories and other records were all false, and had been implanted by some cunning genie to deceive us into believing we had lived a life which actually we had not? There is no way by which we could detect the deception. It is not suggested that memories in general *are* false, but what must be doubtful is whether we do in fact visit the different moments of our life in the correct order. Our only reason for believing we have indeed lived the previous moments is the existence of our memories and other records (and perhaps our wrinkles and grey hairs). If these records have been tampered with, how do we know we are not visiting each of today's moments before yesterday's? Provided yesterday's memories were correctly stacked in the brain we would still feel certain the days succeeded each other in the correct order within the flow of time. This, of course, is nonsense, but it does emphasise the fact that we do not visit the different moments of time in any order at all; they are just *there*. We can form a correct impression of the function of time in our lives only by visualising a static picture like Fig. 4, and must reject the usual moving picture of each day preceding the next.

SUMMARY

To summarise briefly the argument of this chapter, our awareness of a 'present' time is not surprising, for every act of thinking is an 'event' and so occupies a particular point of time, just as our body at that instant occupies a particular position in space. If we consider the world-lines of the memories we hold in the brain, at each instant of time there will be new lines starting, representing the sensations and thoughts we have at that instant, and extending into the future. This steady accumulation of memories as time increases give us the impression of a 'moving' forward of the present, and dictates in which of the two possible time-directions that movement seems to occur.

Almost everything of significance that happens in the universe is irreversible, and the reason for this time-asymmetry cannot be found in the fundamental laws of physics. The explanation was found to lie in the low entropy of the universe, the fact that both thermally and gravitationally it is in an unstable state. This state in turn is due wholly to the world's initial state and its expansion. The recession of the galaxies is seen to be not just an interesting but inconsequential feature of the world; it is the mainspring driving all the processes in the universe, and explaining everything of interest that has ever happened, including the evolution of life itself.

This chapter has attempted to show that belief in a universal 'now', and in the constant moving forward of this 'now', is untenable and fallacious. If this is accepted, then we are presented with a difficult task; everything we do, everything we think, and everything we believe, are so deeply permeated by this concept, that it is very difficult to purge it from our thinking as we consider the problems of philosophy. It requires great vigilance to avoid this impression creeping back into our reasoning, often in the subtlest of ways, as we consider the questions of causation, of free will, of right and wrong, of praise and blame, and of our own intentions and the purpose of the universe. We will inevitably have to continue using the *language* of a moving time as we describe some of the processes around us, for no other language exists, but we must be constantly alert lest this false description plays a part in our argument. Whenever possible we should visualise processes as a static four-dimensional model in space-time rather than as a moving three-dimensional picture. If we fail to avoid this pitfall as we reflect on philosophy's problems then our reasoning will be faulty and our conclusions doubtful.

Chapter 4

CAUSE AND EFFECT

REPEATABILITY AND PREDICTABILITY

The universe is remarkably consistent. Whenever a scientist measures the mass or the electric charge of an electron, or the constant of gravitation, he expects to obtain the same numerical answer; and now that astronomers are observing features at vast distances there seems little reason to doubt that these same values apply throughout the whole of space. A few experts have suggested that such numerical quantities may have changed very slowly over the lifetime of the universe, but there is no evidence for this, and it is generally believed that the characteristics of the individual particles from which matter and radiation are formed, as well as the laws which govern all physical processes, are invariant throughout the whole of space and time.

This consistency explains the high degree of repeatability which phenomena display. A marksman knows that, if he takes careful aim, his shot will strike the target within a few centimetres of its centre. If on some occasion it misses the target altogether he will look for the reason; he may suspect the gun, or the weight or formation of the bullet or the explosive charge which propelled it, or he may seek some reason for his own performance being below standard.

Indeed, in very simple cases, the behaviour of a system is not only repeatable, it is actually predictable. If an astronomer knows the state of the solar system on, say, 1 January 1950, then he is able to calculate the positions of all the major bodies at any date for hundreds of years into the future. Moreover he can do this with sufficient accuracy to describe in detail the track on the earth's surface of any total eclipse of the sun; this requires a knowledge of the moon's position relative to the earth to within a fraction of a mile.

Notice that the process he uses for such calculations is time-reversible. If he can predict an eclipse five hundred years in the future, then he can calculate with equal accuracy the details of one which happened five hundred years ago. It will be pointed out that he does not need to do such calculations for past eclipses; he can look up the details in a history book; and while he cannot be sure that some cataclysm will not engulf the solar system during the next five hundred years and thereby invalidate his calculations, he knows that no such event has occurred during the last five hundred. So although the calculation of past or future events in simple cases is time-symmetric, there appears to be a fundamental asymmetry in matters involving our knowledge, an asymmetry which we will address later in this chapter.

It may be asked just what information our astronomer would need before he could attempt his calculations, whether into the past or the future. In addition to the masses of each of the bodies in the solar system, he would ask for their positions and velocities, i.e. their speeds and direction of travel, at a particular time. The astronomer would then be able to calculate, to whatever degree of accuracy his data allowed, the positions at any time in the future or the past, assuming that no unforeseen events occurred at an intermediate time to upset his results.

Now modern physics teaches us, through the Quantum theory, that these features of repeatability and predictability break down when we are dealing with individual atoms or atomic particles. If we have an atom of radium we know that at some time in the future it will disintegrate radioactively, but we can have no idea when this will happen. On the other hand, if we have a piece of radium big enough to be seen, it must contain many millions of atoms, and we can then be certain that almost exactly one half of these will have disintegrated after sixteen hundred years. We cannot know when a particular atom will disintegrate, but we do know accurately the *probability* that a given atom will split during the next year, and from this we can calculate with precision the time taken for one half to disintegrate provided the number of atoms in our sample is large. It appears that some of the laws of nature are really just statistical laws, and apply only when we are dealing with atoms in large numbers. But this has had no effect on the conceptions of the man in the street, who never deals with atoms in small numbers, and his idea of causality has been formed over the centuries by observing *macroscopic* objects and processes. No further mention of quantum indeterminacy will be made in this chapter, and it will be assumed that we are discussing processes on the scale of everyday observation, the processes which form all our common experiences, and from which we can take examples to examine the cause-effect relationship in detail.

Furthermore, in this chapter we shall not attempt to apply the idea of causation to living beings. Many people believe that the physical laws of causality will never explain the behaviour of human beings, for do we not differ from inanimate objects in that we can determine our own reactions to the situations we find ourselves in? In any case, the workings of the brain of a human or highly developed animal are far too complex to use as illustrations for the simple argument it is hoped to present here. The question of free will is examined in depth in the next chapter; in the present discussion we shall consider only the actions of *macroscopic* and *inanimate* bodies as we attempt to understand the nature of the relationship between what we call *causes* and their *effects* in everyday speech.

THE SPACE-TIME VIEW

If we think of the working of the world as the occurrence of large numbers of events, it is clear that their repeatability and predictability must be the result of a network of linkages between them. Often these links are obvious and clearly seen, as when they take the form of a projectile, or a pulse of radiation, or the change of position of a material body. If the wind dislodges a tile from the top of a building, and the tile then marks the ground where it falls, we can easily see or visualise the linkage between event A, the dislodging of the tile, and event B, the marking of the ground, for it consists of the motion of the tile itself. If event A is an earthquake and event B the destruction of a building some distance away at a slightly later moment, then we have no difficulty picturing the radiation of energy through the ground connecting event A with event B.

Realising that the links between causally connected events consist of the *motion* of material objects, or of some kind of radiated energy, solves many of the traditional problems surrounding the concept of causation. The early philosophers believed these links to be logical – they could be understood just by thinking about them, and without any observations of the real world. David Hume maintained we could never understand them; our knowledge that one event causes another arises only because we frequently see such events occurring together. The interval of time between a cause and its effect provided further difficulty; how can event A cause event B if A no longer exists at the time B occurs? And how can a causal chain occupy a finite time; what was happening between one event and the next? These problems are now all solved; Newton teaches, in opposition to Aristotle, that motion itself requires no cause; only *changes* of speed or direction need explanation. So if the link between events A and B consists of a moving body or a transfer of energy, the time interval between A and B is explained.

It is a further common observation that events do not occur spontaneously. When we find a broken ornament on the floor we blame the children, or the cat. If an unexpected explosion occurs, the police do not rest until they have discovered the event or events which caused the explosion. We say 'There is no effect without a cause'. Viewing this fact in terms of the linkages joining events, we see that every event must be linked to an earlier one, and it follows that all events that have ever happened or ever will happen must all be linked together into one gigantic network, must all be linked, in fact, to the first event of all, the 'big bang' with which the universe came into existence.

In contemplating these relationships between events, we must observe the lessons of Chapter Three and not fall into the trap of regarding time as moving or flowing, with the past determined and immutable while the future is still uncertain and subject to the accidents and whims of today. We should view the whole history of the universe rather as a colossal four-dimensional

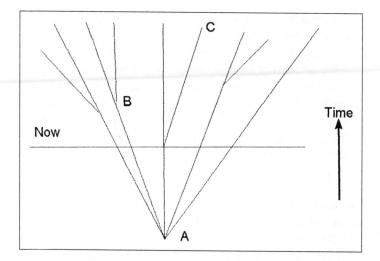

Fig. 5. It is possible to move without back-tracking from A to B and from A to C, but not from B to C. So we say that A and B are causally related, as are A and C, but not B and C.

network of links in space-time joining up every event from the beginning of time to its end. The laws of nature apply strict rules to this network, making it possible in some cases to calculate precisely the linkage structure in one part of space-time when that in a neighbouring part is known. A particular example, and one that seems to us of special importance, is our ability in simple cases to calculate past or future events when we have sufficient information about the state of affairs at one particular moment of time, which on the space-time diagram corresponds to a cross section of four-dimensional space. Only in the simplest cases can we actually perform these calculations, but in many cases where we cannot it does appear that there is sufficient information contained in one cross section to determine uniquely the past and future histories of a part of the universe. For example, we may understand fully the hardware of a computer system and the software in its memory, and it is then theoretically possible to calculate what output will be printed or displayed as the program runs. When this calculation is beyond our powers, we still know that an identical system running an identical program will produce the same results, as will the same computer if we run the same program tomorrow.

Thus even if we cannot calculate the future state of the system from its present state, the *repeatability* of its future action shows that it must be *determined* by the present state.

We say that one event causes another if the two are joined by links in the causal chain in such a way that one can be reached from the other without back-tracking, i.e. proceeding always in the direction of increasing or decreasing time value. Fig. 5 represents on a space-time diagram the linkage connecting a few events. The general form of this diagram will be discussed in later paragraphs, but for the moment let us just notice that event A is linked causally to B, and also to C, for we can travel along the links from A to B or from A to C, without back-tracking. But B cannot be reached from C in this way, and so events B and C are not related causally.

However, this description of what we mean when we say one event causes another is clearly incomplete, for it does not explain why we always apply the word *cause* to the first event, and *effect* to the second one. Why do we believe that the earlier event is responsible for the later, and never the other way round? What is the source of this time-asymmetry? Situations in which time *could* be reversed are conceivable, and a cause would then present an influence on what we call the past. Suppose that, at some time in the future, astronomers observe a body with a mass comparable to the earth's approaching the solar system at high speed from outer space. If it makes a close approach to the earth, the bodies' mutual gravitational attraction will deflect each of them from its course. The earth's orbit around the sun will be altered, and the visiting body might find itself heading more closely towards Mars than if it had not passed so close to the earth. If it then similarly deflects Mars from *its* course before disappearing again into the depths of space, Mars also might have its orbit changed. We would say that the change in Mars' orbit (event B) had been caused by the encounter of the intruding body with the earth (event A). But now let us see how this would look if time were reversed. The bodies would still be moving in accordance with the laws of mechanics and gravitation, and the intruder would approach from the direction in which we previously thought it had vanished, and would firstly change the orbit of Mars (from what we previously thought was its final orbit) and then change the earth's orbit (from what we thought of as *its* final form). The change in the earth's

60

orbit would thus be caused by the encounter with Mars. In this case it seems that cause and effect are interchangeable.

But this sequence of events is unlike any we commonly experience; only in the depths of space can a pair of bodies influence each other's motion without at the same time having some effect on each other's structure. To imagine a situation more like those we commonly observe, suppose this time that the intruding body actually collides with the earth, and shatters it to fragments. Now what happens if we reverse the time direction? Thousands of fragments all come together at the same moment and form two spherical bodies, one of which goes into a circular orbit around the sun while the other calmly retires to the depth of space. This is clearly ridiculous: there can be no question here of cause and effect being interchangeable. The linkage between the events is not itself irreversible; it is the events themselves that make no sense if time is reversed.

Most events *are* irreversible. A bomb explodes, throwing fragments in all directions; fragments never come together to form a bomb. Sugar dissolves in cups of tea when stirred; stirring in the opposite direction does not then restore the sugar to its solid form. Living things grow old, die and decay. In all cases the processes can be seen to involve some form of *dissipation* — the pieces of the exploding bomb fly off in all directions; the molecules of sugar become dissipated throughout the volume of the tea; the complicated fabric of a living being begin to malfunction and lose the special structure we call life — and dissipation is irreversible. In the language of Chapter Three, dissipation represents an increase in entropy, and so the probability of the reverse process ever happening is infinitesimal.

In Chapter Three we discussed the irreversibility of thermal processes; hot bodies cool to the temperature of their surroundings, and this also is a process of dissipation. We saw that these thermal effects are subject to the Second Law of Thermodynamics. It was pointed out that this law is far more general than its name implies, and can be related to any dissipative effect whether or not heat is involved. The law tells us that, left to itself, any set of objects will progress towards its most likely condition, and in this way it is relevant to any situation in which dissipation is involved. If the molecules of an egg are thrown into a room, they are more likely to lie higgledy-piggledy on the floor than to collect into a structure with shell, white and yolk; so a whole egg can easily become a broken one, but the reverse process never happens. A pack of cards is more likely to be in random order than sorted into order, for there are many more arrangements that would be described as 'random' than as 'sorted'; so shuffling a sorted pack will produce a random pack, but shuffling a random pack is unlikely to sort it.

The Second Law of Thermodynamics is sometimes thought to be the most pessimistic piece of knowledge man possesses; it might be likened to the well-known 'Murphy's Law', which says that if something *can* go wrong, it *will* go wrong. Nevertheless its effects are not wholly destructive; some very wonderful and beautiful things happen in the universe, despite the Second Law. The stars and planets have been formed, life has developed on earth and culminated in the evolution of mankind, and man himself has built buildings, painted pictures and composed music. In fact order *can* arise from comparative chaos; the Second Law tells us only that *overall*, the amount of chaos must increase, as the universe moves inexorably towards equilibrium. A good example is provided by the formation of a river. When rain falls on a hillside the drops strike the ground at random, representing a highly disordered state, and yet when they eventually flow into the sea they are collected into a well organised river, all moving the same way, apparently displaying a state of lower entropy. But this is made possible only because of a much greater increase of *gravitational* entropy; the river can form only if the sea is at a lower level than the hills on which the rain falls. The form of the water shows a decrease of entropy, but overall there has to be an increase, which we see if we take account of the downward component of the river's progress towards the sea.

The natural state of the Universe, its most probable state, would be that in which entropy was at its highest possible level so that apart from occasional, slight random fluctuations, nothing much would ever happen. There would be nothing we could describe as an 'event'. For us it is fortunate that the world is not yet in that state; it is full of objects with differing temperatures, and gravitating bodies which are still separated. With such a high degree of complexity and organisation around us it is not surprising that almost all the events we observe involve some dissipation. The energy of a falling tile lies in the fact that all its parts are moving downwards at the same speed; but when it hits the ground this energy is all dissipated into the random vibrations of its millions of molecules and those of the surrounding ground, as the organised energy of descent becomes the disorganised energy of heat. This continual dissipation throws a new light onto the structure of the linkage of events discussed in previous paragraphs. The structure must be, in fact, a diagramatical tree, as illustrated in Fig. 5, with repeated branching as one looks higher on the diagram. In making a drawing such as this, one must be careful not to mark or imagine an *arrow* on each link, to show which event is the cause of the other, for this would be tacitly assuming a directionality for the causative effect. There is no difficulty marking the direction of *time*. The time arrow must point upwards, for it is in the direction of later time that dissipation increases, and the Universe proceeds relentlessly towards greater and greater chaos, towards a state of ever increasing probability.

The diagram shows that at later times the number of events continually increases, but the significance of each is less and less. The fall of a stone is more important than the random motion of a single molecule. There are exceptions to this general rule, and it is not difficult to point to small events in the past that have triggered major cataclysms, but this is rare. If the Universe finally reaches a state of equilibrium then hardly ever will an event occur of more significance than the collision of two molecules.

THE TIME-ASYMMETRY OF CAUSE AND EFFECT

We can now throw light on the irreversibility of cause and effect. If at some time in the future we are considering the events shown in Fig. 5, we shall know that events A and B both happened, and that they were linked causally. But let us consider the situation as

63

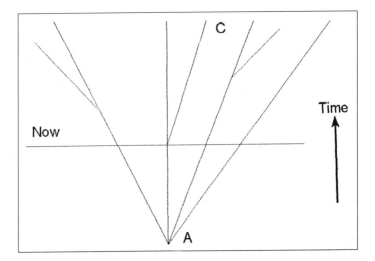

Fig. 6. An observer at time 'Now' knows that A has happened, but believes (falsely) that B may not happen.

seen by an observer at a time *between* the occurrence of events A and B, at the moment represented by the 'Now' line in the diagram. As was mentioned in the last chapter, and as we shall soon demonstrate, memories, like all records, can only represent *past* events, so at the time marked 'Now', records or memories of A may exist, but not of event B. We feel that the occurrence of event B is not a certainty; our observer can envisage a world (wrongly, as it happens) in which event B does not exist, as shown in Fig. 6. Notice that in this drawing we have had to erase not only B, but also all the events *linked* to B, for otherwise these would be unconnected to the main stream, they would be 'events without a cause'. So our observer can doubt whether B, along with all its effects, will occur, but is unable to doubt the occurrence of event A, for all around him are events linked to A, these being represented on our diagram by points on the 'Now' line. If he doubts the occurrence of A he is surrounded by events which have lost their link with the rest of creation and so have no cause. Suppose A represents a cricket bat striking a ball, and B represents that ball breaking a window in a nearby house. The 'Now' line represents a moment in time *after* the ball has been struck but *before* it hits the window. Our observer is unable to know whether the ball will break the window, and can visualise the possibility both of its doing so and of its not doing so. The second of these two pictures is in fact wrong, but he cannot know this. One thing he can *not* accept is the non-occurrence of A, for this is an event he actually saw and heard happening. Some of the light waves reflected by the ball as it was hit entered his eye, and some of the sound waves generated entered his ear, and memories of each exist in his brain; these were some of the dissipative effects linked to event A, as shown on the diagram. He therefore believes that A 'has occurred' and cannot be undone, whereas he thinks (incorrectly) that B may not occur.

Here then is the source of the directionality of cause and effect. When our 'Now' line is between two events (A and B) there is distinct asymmetry between the knowledge we can have of the two, and we have come to believe that this asymmetry lies actually in the linkage of B to A rather than in our own brains. We believe that the line representing the linkage should have an arrow on it. This impression is so strong that when, at a later time after B has occurred, and there is now no such asymmetry in our knowledge of the two events, we still think the link itself was asymmetrical, and we say A *caused* B.

THE TIME-ASYMMETRY OF
MEMORIES AND RECORDS

We should now be able to understand a matter which so far has been glossed over, namely why memories, and all other types of record, can only be of past events. A record is always caused by the event it records. In general the event will have many other effects along with the creation of its record; at the very least the event must have *one* other effect, for otherwise the record would be of nothing but itself. The process of recording can be seen as just a part of the dissipation associated with the event, and so must come after it in time. Here is the explanation we seek of the fact that memories and records can exist only of past events, and never of future ones.

It might be thought that the creation of a record contravenes the law of increasing entropy, for the essential feature of a record is that its structure is a copy or a representation of some aspect of the events it records. When you photograph a scene the pattern of darkened areas on the negative bears a recognisable relationship to the objects being photographed; when a barograph records the varying air pressure there is a clear relationship between the position of the pen and the value it represents. It seems that the generating of a record actually *increases* the amount of order in the Universe, for the record copies some of the structure of the thing it represents without destroying any of that structure. However, the Second Law of Thermodynamics cannot be broken so easily, and we know that the appearance of this extra structure must be accompanied by the loss of at least as much order in other forms or places. The camera works only because some of the highly organised energy of the sun or flash-gun is dissipated as light and lost for ever; the barograph works only because some of the ink collected together in its pen is smeared irreversibly onto the chart. Even the formation of a memory is possible only because the brain is part of a living body which must consume food containing complex forms of chemical energy, all derived ultimately from sunlight, and dissipates this energy in the form of heat at a much lower temperature than the sun's, so that it can never again be converted into chemical energy.

SUMMARY

To summarise, it is our observation of the *consistency* of the world and the *repeatability* of processes which leads us to conclude that events are linked together in an understandable way. The fact that spontaneous events do not seem to occur shows us that this linkage must embrace everything that happens in the world. Because we live in a low-entropy universe, almost every event results in a change to a more probable state, which in effect means a process of dissipation, and so the linkage of events must form a tree structure. Part of this dissipation may consist of the formation of records or memories of events, so that at any moment in time an observer has evidence of past events, which he says 'have occurred, and cannot be undone', but has no such firm evidence of future events which he says 'may not occur'. This asymmetry prompts him to believe that, of the two events at the ends of a link, that at the earlier end is more certain than that at the other end, while in reality it is only his knowledge of the two events which differs in certainty. He calls the earlier event a *cause*, and the later one an *effect*.

We have excluded from our discussion events on the very small scale of atomic particles, and events involving the behaviour of conscious beings. The first of these restrictions does not invalidate or modify any of the conclusions reached so far as they apply to macroscopic processes except for the remote and rare possibility that some macroscopic events may be caused by events on the atomic scale. The second restriction makes it essential to consider now whether the same laws of cause and effect which we have discussed in their application to inanimate matter do in fact apply also to conscious animals and humans, and this we do in the next chapter.

Chapter 5

FREE WILL

THE FREE WILL ARGUMENT

Are we really free to determine our own behaviour? Do we differ
fundamentally from machines, whose actions are governed
completely by their mechanism and the signals they receive from
the outside world, rather than their own volition? Of the questions
asked by philosophers this is one of the oldest, and one of the
most important; if two thinking people disagree in their answers
to it then their philosophies are likely to diverge over a wide
area.

A scientist believing that everything can ultimately be
explained by the laws of nature leaves no room for a non-material
mind to direct human behaviour. This must all be determined by
the physics and chemistry of the human brain and body; freedom
of the will must be an illusion. On the other hand, most Christians
today believe that man's will is free. Although the argument has
sometimes been clouded by the doctrine of predestination,
whereby God has determined in advance which human souls are
to be rewarded in the after-life, most schools of Christian doctrine
teach that we are free to follow a good or an evil course as we
wish, expecting finally to be held responsible before our Maker
for the lives we have led.

Such divergence of belief seems surprising in a question so
close to the centre of everyone's thinking. Throughout our waking
lives we are making decisions and planning our next actions;
how can there be any room for disagreement over a process with
which we are so familiar? And yet, in the light of what was said

in an earlier chapter about the way our experience deceives us in our beliefs and understanding when we probe our innermost thoughts, perhaps it is not so surprising; we might expect the mind to offer us false clues and to send us on bogus trails when we try to investigate the decision-making process, for this is right at the heart of the mind itself.

DETERMINISM

Those who believe in a purely mechanistic explanation of human behaviour are often said to support the doctrine of *determinism*. The word was much used by scientists at the end of the nineteenth century. They were having notable success in understanding the way the world behaved. They used their knowledge to make accurate predictions of the type mentioned in the last chapter, where the number of independent bodies was small, and the exact future movement of each could be calculated from the laws of mechanics and gravitation as in the Solar System. They were also building machines, and optical and electrical equipment, of ever increasing complexity, whose performance they could predict while the ideas were still on the drawing board. Even the biologist was beginning to understand the mechanism of evolution, and to believe the development of living things also had followed the universal rules of cause and effect. Human behaviour alone remained unpredictable, but many scientists maintained that eventually man's activity would also be found to obey the immutable laws of physics and chemistry, even if the complexity of the higher life forms precludes any exact prediction of their actions. It was believed that the laws of nature were almost fully understood, and that they applied to all events throughout the universe, even those involving human thought and action.

It might be asked whether the free will question can be settled by means of scientific experiment. If the question really is meaningful, surely it must make some difference to the way people behave, a difference which should be observable experimentally. Most experiments are conducted by carefully establishing a set of initial conditions, setting some process into action, and then observing the outcome. In many cases this outcome is found to be determined uniquely by the initial conditions, giving evidence of a causal relationship; could we not apply this method to some simple example of human activity, and thereby discover whether or not man's actions are determined in the same way? There are essentially four possible methods whereby the results of an experiment can be shown to be determined causally by its initial conditions, but unfortunately, for a variety of reasons, not one of these methods can be applied to an investigation of human behaviour. The first method is illustrated in experiments where we understand each stage of a process, and knowing it to be causally connected to the preceding and following stages allows us to deduce that the whole process must also be deterministic; to apply this method to problems of human behaviour would require an understanding of every stage of the decision-making process within the brain, an understanding we are unlikely ever to possess. Secondly, we might be able to predict reliably an experimental result, showing it to be deterministic even when we cannot follow in detail the causative chain it is pursuing, but again human behaviour is far too complex for us ever to have sufficient knowledge to make infallible predictions in this case. A third experimental method involves performing many identical tests simultaneously, as when a large number of atoms take part in some particular chemical process and all react in the same way, showing the reaction to be deterministic. However, we cannot apply this method to humans, for, unlike atoms, no two humans are the same; all too frequently, when a large number of people are subject to the same stimuli, some behave in one way and some in another. Even identical twins must have had slightly different upbringing; if it is found that such twins sometimes respond differently in identical situations this provides no argument against the deterministic philosophy, for the difference may result from some subtle divergence between the natures of the twins. Finally, we can often perform the same experiment many times *in succession*, as when we run the same program repeatedly on a computer and observe the same output each time; but again we cannot apply this method to human behaviour, for it is impossible to ensure the initial state is the same each time. The fact that a human subject has met a particular stimulus previously may in itself account for a different response the second time, forbidding us from attributing such a difference to the subject's exercising his will. It therefore seems impossible to discover by experimental methods whether human activity is purely the result of causal processes, and we must resort to a less direct approach if we are to resolve the free will question.

At the start of the twentieth century most scientists did believe both the inanimate and the living worlds to be controlled by deterministic laws; but then within a few years not one but two revolutions hit the scientific community: Einstein's theory of relativity and Planck's quantum theory, and each of these demanded a reappraisal of many of the scientists' traditional beliefs. Both theories were established by 1905, and they shattered in particular the rather cosy world of the physicists, some of whom had believed their work to be almost finished, a complete understanding being within their grasp of all the laws of nature. We will not attempt to explain either of these theories here, but one aspect of the quantum theory, the 'Uncertainty Principle' of Heisenberg (1901-1976), is of importance in our present discussion, for it shows surprisingly that when dealing with atomic particles the laws of physics are *not* themselves deterministic; many of the predictions that can be made about such particles are no more than mathematical probabilities, as was mentioned briefly in Chapter Four. Although we know accurately the probability that the atom of radium mentioned in that chapter will disintegrate on a given day, we have no idea on which particular day it will actually happen; and the remarkable aspect of this, as believed by most physicists, is that the uncertainty is not due to our own imperfect knowledge of the situation – as our imperfect knowledge of the movement of a spinning coin prevents us from predicting on which side it will fall – but is an intrinsic absence of certainty within the atom itself. When we have a large number of such particles, we can predict how many will divide on a given day, just as when we spin a large number of coins we know that very nearly one half will come down showing 'heads'. Only when dealing with atomic particles in small numbers can the indeterminacy be observed; whenever we have matter in the quantities to which we are accustomed it still behaves (very

7 1

nearly) deterministically. But science was forced to acknowledge that believing all the world's activity to be determined by inflexible laws had been a major error; the rules governing the event linkage described in Chapter Four, at any rate at the atomic level, do not, after all, permit calculation of the future (or past) state of a system from knowledge of its state at the present. Although this did not greatly affect the behaviour of macroscopic systems, where the statistical laws of the atomic realm generate laws of almost complete certainty because of the immense numbers involved, nevertheless it became necessary to reconsider the contribution that science thought it had made to the free will argument.

THE EVIDENCE OF HUMAN BEHAVIOUR

We all conduct our daily lives, and relate to other people, as if we *are* responsible for our decisions and actions. We praise our friends when they do well and criticise them when they do badly. We sometimes have to agonise over a decision, and when our choices turn out to be successful we are glad we made them, and when less successful we wish we had chosen otherwise. We train our children to distinguish right from wrong, and to be truthful and honest, and we encourage them to strive hard at tasks which yield little present satisfaction in order to achieve rewards in the future.

On the other hand there is no doubt that much of our behaviour *is* governed by laws of cause and effect. The actions of the soldier on parade are determined precisely by the Sergeant Major, the clothing we put on is determined by the weather, we get out of bed when the alarm clock rings and we jump out of the way if we see a car heading towards us. It may be that the soldier is free to disobey his orders, or we to wear summer clothing in winter, stay in bed all day or stand our ground in the face of an approaching car, but these things do not usually happen. Most of our behaviour involves no element of personal decision-making. Even if we have the capacity to exercise our will over everything we do, we often have no need to do so; our actions are determined by the circumstances. Where personal choice *is* involved we can often find reasons for our decisions; the soldier may desert because his wife is ill, we can stay in bed if we feel unwell and we might stand in front of a car if we are depressed and suicidal. Even the actions of the criminal are often explained in terms of his present circumstances or upbringing, and those of the eccentric as due to his unconventional character. By finding a reason for each of these unexpected forms of behaviour are we not in effect admitting they are *determined* by something, and thereby removing the need to enlist free will as an explanation?

RANDOM BEHAVIOUR

The working of a digital computer is necessarily deterministic; whenever the same input is applied then the same output is produced. In theory an expert should be able to calculate what that output will be, but when this is not possible we still know the process is deterministic because it is *repeatable*, and always produces the same results.

If the computer is faulty, then this might appear no longer to be true, for running the same program under identical conditions may indeed give different results. But if we fully understood the nature of the fault would we not still be able to predict the machine's output? In practice we would probably say the results were influenced by a random element in the same way that the result of tossing a coin or rolling a dice is random. But the use of the word *random* is incorrect in each of these contexts; we are unable to predict the computer's behaviour only because we do not fully understand the nature of its fault; we do not know whether the coin will land heads or tails, or which number the dice will indicate, only because we do not know all the facts about their initial motion or the forces at work on them as they move. If we could have all the facts we wanted (and a great deal more calculating facility than we possess at present) we should be able to calculate each of these results. To express it differently, if we could ensure identical initial conditions then once again the performance of our computer, coin or dice would be repeatable. We use the word *random* almost always in situations where we ought not to; we are referring to our own ignorance rather than any intrinsic indeterminacy in the system we are describing. An exception is provided by the sub-atomic phenomena described earlier, in which it is impossible to have sufficient knowledge to make exact predictions; such events are sometimes essentially undetermined. This makes it possible to imagine a situation in which a computer's output may *really* be random. Suppose the machine had an incipient fault so delicately poised that whether or not it occurred depended on the behaviour of a single atom; then the output might indeed have a random element. We would be able to say truthfully that the results of running the program were not determined by the initial conditions. It seems unlikely that such a fault ever occurs in practice, but any computer's performance must either be deterministic or contain a random element. There can be no third alternative. If its output is not determined by the initial conditions (taking into account any faults) then that output is random.

HUMAN BEHAVIOUR: THE THREE ALTERNATIVES

So we must ask whether all human behaviour is determined in the same way as that of a fault-free computer, whether it sometimes incorporates a random element as might a faulty computer, or whether perhaps there is some third factor to consider, an element of freedom which is essentially lacking in a computer. Psychology teaches us that the springs of our action are often complex, so that we cannot expect always to understand the causes of our behaviour. When we make a decision there may be many conflicting factors at work, some conscious and some unconscious, some rational and some irrational, some relating to the external situation and some to our own nature, past experience, hopes and fears. Is it not possible that the most powerful of these eventually determines the action we take? Might not our actions be governed by all the conflicting influences at work within the brain in the same way that a material body responds to the forces acting on it?

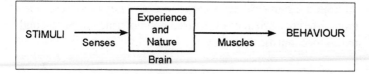

Fig. 7. The relationship between the Senses, the Brain, and the Muscles, as seen from a Determinist's viewpoint.

In most situations we are indeed pushed this way and that by the forces at work on us, as illustrated by the soldier on parade or the pedestrian jumping to avoid the car. Our behaviour depends partly upon our nature and experience, but is chiefly a response to the stimuli to which we are subject, even though it appears to us that we are really in control. In some circumstances we may suspect that a random element enters into our decision-making, an element with no cause and no reason; we all know people who are particularly unpredictable and erratic. But this does little to advance the present argument, for random behaviour is essentially aimless, and does not illustrate what we mean by freedom of the will.

Much more important is the belief that, when we exert our will, we are able to *override* the causal elements in our behaviour, bringing into play a new force to work in conjunction with the deterministic and random effects. For the Ancients, the problem was less puzzling; man's actions were not unique in being determined by his acts of will; the succession of the seasons, the flowing of a river and the movements of the heavenly bodies were all evidence that these things had souls of their own, or were subject to the will of the gods. Today it is different; we now know that most of nature is governed not by its own wishes or the whims of the gods, but by inflexible laws. If there are any exceptions they are confined to humans and some animals. Those who believe we have a freedom transcending nature's laws must now justify their doctrine as rigorously as their materialistic opponents need to justify theirs.

The materialist might start his argument with a little drawing (Fig. 7) to show the stimuli reaching a person's brain via the nerves of his five senses, the many factors in the decision-making process being broadly categorised as *experience* and *nature*, and the resulting behaviour being implemented by

7 5

appropriate signals to the person's muscles. Let us now consider how different advocates of the free will doctrine might respond to this mechanistic description.

FREE WILL:

THE ARGUMENTS IN SUPPORT

The first might say simply, 'I know I make my own decisions.' No-one need disagree with this; these decisions could still be made deterministically by the complex mechanism of the brain.

A second might expand on this a little, and say, 'My *mind* makes decisions, and governs the behaviour of my body.' Again this need not be a cause for disagreement. The speaker might have a picture of a non-physical mind interacting with the brain, but if we reject this interpretation we are still at liberty to use the word 'mind' to describe the deepest areas of the brain itself, and in particular those areas which weigh and respond to the various pressures determining our behaviour.

A third response might be, 'I know I can affect the future by my decisions, and so they cannot depend wholly on the laws of physics and chemistry, whereby the future is uniquely determined.' Now this argument is false, for we can easily find examples of processes which affect the future even in situations where we know the future *is* determined. The arrival into the solar system of a body from outer space discussed in the last chapter is a case in point; the influence of the earth on this body as it made its near approach clearly affected the future behaviour of Mars, and yet the situation is perfectly pre-determined. A mathematician equipped with knowledge of the past history of the bodies concerned could calculate with certainty the new orbits of the earth and Mars and the intruding body. Our decisions do indeed affect the future, for they are among the events linked to those in the future, but this is not an argument in favour of those decisions being 'free'.

A fourth person may say, 'When I have made a decision, I know I *could* have decided differently.' This is a more formidable objection, but its lack of precision makes it easier to refute. We must ask whether the speaker means, 'I could have acted differently if the circumstances had differed slightly,' or 'I could have acted differently even if all the circumstances had been the same.' Suppose two similar situations *had* arisen, and the subject *had* decided differently on the two occasions; what would be his response if we asked, '*Why* did you act differently the second time?' He would be quite likely to find a reason, even if it were only, 'Because I felt like it!' But is this not a change of circumstance? The second situation differed from the first in respect of the subject's feelings, and so the outcome was different, just as we would expect in a wholly deterministic environment. On the other hand, suppose he said, 'I don't know why I acted differently. There was no reason.' Is not this just saying that the choice was random? As explained above a purely random choice is not an example of what most people mean by free will. It must be agreed that the concept of free will becomes increasingly elusive as we scrutinise it more intently.

Finally, our fifth debater might simply declare, 'I know my mind is a *non-material* agency; it is with this that I make my decisions. The mind then acts on my brain in a manner that defies the laws of science, and thereby determines my actions.' Despite the great progress they have made in recent years, physiologists are not in a position to assert without doubt that the whole brain, including its deepest recess, is governed by the universal laws of physics. Recent studies do give a clear picture of stimuli arriving at our sense organs, travelling along nerves to particular areas of the brain, and producing specific reactions. Signals then pass from other areas of the brain to our muscles and cause the various aspects of our behaviour. Yet no-one has been able to explain what happens in between; if an advocate of free will maintains that there is a supernatural agent somewhere in the chain — a stage in the process which does not obey the rules governing the rest of the Universe — a counter-argument is difficult to find. However, even if we do admit this possibility, we still cannot escape the choice between a wholly deterministic explanation of human behaviour, and one in which the non-causal elements are merely random. Although we may accept the possibility of a 'ghost in the machine', the following paragraphs attempt to show that we still have no meaningful alternative to a picture of human activity governed completely by deterministic rules, even if these are not necessarily the rules of physical science.

FREE WILL:
THE THIRD ALTERNATIVE

Let us digress for a while from the main argument. When an engineer designs a bridge, one of the simple principles he uses is the knowledge that, if it is not to collapse, all the forces on it must balance. If he knows the total weight of the bridge then the total upward force of the supports must equal this downward weight. The great value of this method is that he can apply it not only to the bridge as a whole but to any of its parts, such as one-half of the bridge, or one girder, or one rivet. Applying it to a single rivet teaches him something about the forces in the elements this rivet holds together. But when he applies it to the whole bridge he can ignore all the many internal forces, for these each act in two opposing directions and cancel each other out, leaving only the external forces for him to consider. If, after designing the bridge, he wishes to calculate what increase there will be in the stresses on the supports and anchorages when a vehicle of known weight is standing on its deck, he could do this by finding the additional forces on the girders immediately under the vehicle, then the forces exerted on the structure supporting these girders, and so on, until ultimately he finds the effect on the main supports of the bridge. It would be much easier, however, to consider the vehicle as part of the bridge, and calculate the forces needed to support the whole system, bridge and vehicle, regarded as a single entity. This method would tell him nothing of the extra internal forces within the structure, but would give the external forces with far less effort.

This presents a good analogy to the way a person's behaviour depends upon his circumstances. The influences which act on us from outside and our eventual responses to them are represented by the external forces on the bridge, while the processes at work within our bodies and brains correspond to

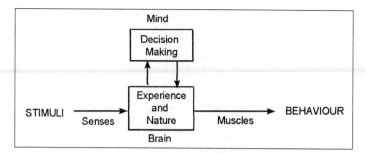

Fig 8. The relationship between Mind and Body, from the point of
view of one who believes we exercise our free will by means
of our non-material mind.

internal forces. If we believe in a non-material mind influencing
the brain, this is portrayed by some additional external force on
the bridge, such as the weight of the vehicle. Let us now consider
the *whole* structure, the body, the nervous system, the brain and
the mind (if you believe it exists separately). Within this
framework are all the tendencies that a person was born with,
all the influences he has ever experienced, all his memories, the
knowledge he has acquired and the character he has developed
over the years. There is a constant input of stimuli from his
sense organs, and the output consists of his actions and behaviour,
as shown in Fig. 7. Now do we believe that those actions are
caused by his character and sense inputs, or do we not? In other
words, if we could know everything about his nature, his every
experience since birth, and his present stimuli, and we
understood perfectly the mechanism of his body and brain, would
we have enough information to determine his reactions to these
stimuli in the same way that the output of a computer is
determined by its initial state and input? If we do not, the
only alternative is to ascribe to them a *random* element, as we
agreed might be the case when referring to a faulty computer
system. 'No,' you may protest, 'that is *not* the only alternative!
When I make a decision *I* influence my brain. If I disagree with
my natural reactions to a situation then I intervene, and decide
for myself what response to make.' And you would support your
protest with a drawing like Fig. 8, showing how your mind
receives information from the brain, makes its own decisions,
and transmits these back to the brain. However, this is not the

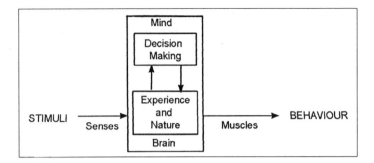

Fig. 9. We can consider the whole structure, Body, Brain and Mind
    as a single entity.

way we agreed to look at the problem. We are considering the
response of the *whole* system, body, brain and mind. I would
respond to your diagram by drawing a box around the whole
structure, as in Fig. 9, and would ask again the same question,
'Do we believe that the behaviour of this *whole* entity is caused
by its stimuli or do we not, for again the only alternative is a
random element as in a faulty computer?' You cannot protest
that your behaviour comes into neither category because of your
'acts of will', for the will is within the system we are considering;
if it plays a part in determining your actions then its contribution
must be represented by reactions within the box, even if its
influence is of a non-material or a non-scientific nature. The action
of your hypothetical mind on the brain is like the pressure of the
vehicle on the bridge; if you wish, you can consider how it reacts
with the brain as the engineer could calculate the vehicle's reaction
with the roadway, but I prefer to consider the whole person, as
the engineer considered the bridge and vehicle as a whole, when
discussing the reaction of that person to his stimuli. If we rule out
any random element in our behaviour, then whether or not we
believe in a non-material mind, we are driven to the conclusion
that our behaviour *is* wholly determined by our brain and the
stimuli we receive via the senses. The linkage between these
stimuli and our reactions to them is obviously complex, and some
stages within that linkage may possibly be non-physical, in that
they might not be governed by the rules which apply to the whole
of the non-living Universe, but your argument gains nothing by
asserting that this is so, for the part played by the non-material

element must be of the same nature as that of the material elements in the chain of causation. If there is a causal relationship between the 'input' to, and 'output' from, a human being, it seems simpler to assume that this springs from those same rules which govern the behaviour of the inanimate world. So while we are not arguing that the existence of the non-material mind has been disproved, if asserting its existence adds nothing to our understanding surely the wiser course is to dispense with it.

Some writers have attempted to use the quantum uncertainty principle as a loophole whereby a non-material mind may break the causal chain and influence the material brain without infringing the universal laws of physics. As explained above, when dealing with single atomic particles, or very small numbers of them, a strictly deterministic relationship between events no longer applies. It seems unlikely that pieces of the brain small enough for causality to break down in this way could have sufficient effect on other parts of the brain for our behaviour to be influenced thereby, but the idea must be taken seriously, for we are familiar with situations in which small causes can ultimately produce vast effects. An engine driver can start the movement of hundreds of tons of train by moving a lever, a small spark can initiate a mighty explosion, a single accidental act can start a major war which influences the course of history. A single atom of the brain, therefore, could possibly undergo a change of energy level that is not in itself subject to the laws of cause and effect, but which initiates a causal chain in other parts of the brain, and influences our behaviour. Perhaps in some way the *mind* is able to bring about such an event, and single atoms provide the link through which, in intelligent living beings, the mind can influence the body. But further reflection shows that this proposition does not advance the argument any further, for the reasoning of the previous paragraphs, as illustrated by Fig. 9, does not depend on the *form* taken by the reactions between mind and brain. These reactions may be simple physical and chemical effects, they may involve non-material influences, or they may include non-deterministic atomic events, but we are still left with only our first two alternatives; either our behaviour is *caused* by the stimuli we receive or it is *random*. So if we exclude random and aimless influences the only alternative is a decision-making process which is wholly deterministic; if we could know everything about a person we would be able to predict his response to the stimuli he receives throughout life.

Further weight is added to this argument by taking on board the teaching of Chapter Three. We saw there how the idea of a *moving* time, with a universal 'now' constantly progressing from past to future, and the false impression that the past is fixed while the future is still uncertain, can lead to erroneous conclusions. The only way to free ourselves from this blinkered view is to picture the world as a four dimensional linkage of events, with no privileged cross section corresponding to 'now', and no fundamental distinction between those events which lie in the future and those in the past. This clearly affects the present discussion, for our impressions of freedom depend wholly on a belief that we have control over the future but not the past; if the distinction between the past and the future is purely subjective, with no significance in the outside world, how can we subscribe to a process which affects the one but not the other? The apparent asymmetry between the past and the future is due wholly to our having memories of the past only. If the distinction does not really exist, and if indeed the dividing line between the two time regions is only in the minds of individuals, then it does not make sense to assert that we can affect the future but not the past. If living creatures did have some means of tampering with the causal linkage of the world outside themselves, there is no way this could change future events from what they would otherwise have been without also changing past events. No meaning can be found for 'free will' compatible with this picture of the world.

THE IMPRESSION OF FREEDOM

If this view is correct, why then do we have so compelling a belief that we *are* able to pursue our own course, to over-rule the forces at work within us by our own will-power? This feeling is never more in evidence than when we have some traumatic experience requiring the making of agonising decisions. We see our neighbour's house on fire and suspect there may be someone trapped inside with little time left for rescue. Do we ignore the dangers and go into the house, or do we follow a safer but less praiseworthy course such as going away to call for help? There will be many influences at work within the brain clamouring to be satisfied. Throughout our lives we have been taught to admire altruistic and self-sacrificing behaviour; in less desperate circumstances we have formed habits of thoughtfulness and kindness; we have developed *principles* which guide us through difficult experiences without our having to consider afresh the issues raised each time a challenging situation arises. On the other hand the instinct of self-preservation and the fear of injury drive us away from danger. We can easily imagine these conflicting tendencies at work within the brain, each demanding to be obeyed. Is it surprising that we feel stressed, and believe we ourselves have the onerous responsibility of making a decision rather than witnessing a conflict in which we have no part?

Our ability to predict the outcome of each course of action is the factor which raises our decision-making process above that of the lower animals. We can visualise the satisfaction we would derive, and the praise and gratitude we would experience after a successful rescue of our neighbour, and criticism we would receive if we ran away, but also the possible pain and injury we might suffer in the burning building. This capacity to use our intelligence to foresee the consequences of different courses of action is another powerful force at work in deciding which one we follow. It is not quite true to say that this ability to predict outcomes is unique to humans; a computer can play a very reasonable game of chess, which it does by working through all the possible courses the game may take for each of the moves it can legally make, and choosing that which will lead to its greatest advantage several moves ahead. It is not suggested that a computer engaged in a game is *aware* of the decisions it makes, but if it were, would it not believe it was making its own decisions, that it was winning its games by the exercise of its will? What is the difference in principle between its decision-making process and that which we employ?

Another factor contributing to the widespread belief that the mind has a mystical control over the body is the essential dualism of the culture within which Westerners have grown up during the past few centuries. This is emphasised by the Christian doctrine which, not only in overtly Christian communities, has formed the basis for our traditional morality, and of the upbringing of our young. We are taught not to take the easy course in those situations where 'the spirit indeed is willing, but the flesh is weak' (Matthew 26: 41), implicitly acknowledging the dichotomy between spirit and flesh, and the influence of the one over the other. If we believe in a mind which transcends the limitations of time and space, and still more if we believe in man's immortal soul, it is easy to overlook the inconsistencies of a philosophy which ascribes our behaviour to the whims of a personal will.

SUMMARY

To summarise this chapter, our views on the freedom of the human will must be central to our beliefs concerning many other fundamental philosophical questions. In the early years of the twentieth century science seemed to favour a deterministic explanation of everything including human behaviour; present opinion is once again divided, but the thinking is often muddled. There appear to be three possible factors involved in decision making: a purely deterministic process of cause and effect, an element of randomness, and the non-deterministic action of our will. But when we attempt to specify precisely what this third possibility really means it vanishes before our view. Whereas we treat people as if they *are* responsible for their decisions, nevertheless they seem always ready to justify them, and so to imply that they *had* a reason, and therefore that their decisions were, after all, the outcome of some causal chain. Although this provides no proof that the laws governing the working of the brain are the same as those governing everything else in the Universe, nothing seems to be gained by imagining them otherwise. If the impression that we can transcend the rule of cause and effect in our decision-making is indeed false, nonetheless we can easily understand how the illusion arises, for the tendencies that compete within the brain in making difficult decisions are many and complex.

Chapter 6

HUMAN BEHAVIOUR AND MORALS

PRAISE AND BLAME

Certain aspects of our behaviour are easily explained within a deterministic framework of belief. Much of our conduct is attributable directly or indirectly to the influence of the instincts with which we were born, often supplemented by our memories of the past and our predictions of the future. We naturally look for food when we are hungry, and our memory assists us in knowing where to find it, perhaps by reminding us of the location of our favourite restaurant. Moreover we can lay plans today that should ensure we have enough to eat in the days ahead, perhaps by visiting our local grocery shop.

When we examine more complex forms of behaviour, however, we quickly encounter situations in which our motivation is not so easy to explain. Even when hungry, we do not help ourselves to food belonging to other people, for we know we *ought* not to steal; we may sometimes strive to ensure other people less fortunate than ourselves are fed while we go hungry, for we know we *should* be generous to those in need. What meaning can we attach to words such as 'ought' and 'should' if we are describing the action of a mere machine? How can a machine, however complex, have features of *generosity* or *responsibility* built into its mechanism?

In our contacts with other people we always treat them as if they are personally responsible for their actions. This is particularly true when we deal with young folk as they grow up, for we believe that in teaching them the elements of good behaviour we are helping them make right decisions in later life. If we ourselves have been well trained in our earlier years we claim to have a set of moral precepts within which we try to live our lives; we know the difference between right and wrong. We think it just that our country should have laws to deter its less responsible citizens from wrong-doing, and we are in favour of criminals being punished, for we believe they know their actions to be unacceptable. They should, and could, behave better. But if a criminal's lawyer convinces a judge that a crime was not committed deliberately, we expect a more lenient sentence; now, if we have convinced ourselves that all our actions are determined by inflexible rules and not by our own wilfulness, does it not mean that *all* criminals should be treated leniently, for surely none can be said to act deliberately?

Then again, we are impressed by those who devote a part of their lives to helping others, and by those who behave generously or heroically. We admire one who rushes into a stormy sea to rescue a child, and we wish to see him rewarded with a testimonial or a medal. Is this rational if we believe that his actions were wholly determined by a causal chain, rather than by his own volition? On the other hand, when we meet someone who is lazy and feckless, how do we reply if he demands, 'Why should I bother myself with unpleasant or dangerous tasks? Why should I try to be helpful, or to do my job well, or to resist temptations? If my behaviour is all determined by forces outside my control, I may as well save myself the effort and allow fate to take its course'?

THE EVOLUTION OF BEHAVIOUR

These questions suggest that the philosophy we are advocating fails to explain many of the ways in which people react together in modern society. If free will is no more than the working out of causal laws, what right have we to blame or punish wrong-doers, or to expect them to behave better? What reason have we to struggle with difficult circumstances, or our own lethargy, if our actions are determined by the laws of nature, and not by our efforts? What point is there in correcting our children's behaviour if they lack the freedom to improve it? The rest of this chapter attempts to show that these apparent contradictions are not real; a belief that our behaviour is caused in the same way as the behaviour of inanimate objects does not absolve us from blame when we behave badly, nor relieve us of responsibility to train our children and to apply the principles of justice in our society.

To set the scene, let us examine the role played by evolution in the development of man, and in the growth of society and civilisation. The Darwinian concept of 'survival' can explain fully the early development of plants, which became increasingly complex as they adapted more successfully to their environment. When the first animals appeared, and creatures evolved which needed to search for food, it was necessary for several *instincts* to appear. An organism that was not permanently rooted in a source of nourishment had to be able to move, to feed and to reproduce, and the actions needed to accomplish these tasks had to be coded and stored permanently in a rudimentary form of brain. Along with this development was the gradual emergence of sense organs by which the brain could be given information about the creature's environment, the presence of food, a potential mate, or some danger, and the brain had to grow in complexity so that it could respond to the ever-increasing volume of data supplied by the senses.

An important stage in the process was the development of a sense of *pleasure* and *pain*. This represents a clever bit of 'programming' whereby a single area of the brain, a 'pleasure' centre, would encourage the continuance of activities such as feeding, mating or basking in the sun, and a 'pain' centre would encourage movement away from irritating stimuli, such as thorns or a cold wind. Whether or not an organism at this stage was actually *aware* of its pleasures and pains is a different matter; we will consider the question of *consciousness* in a later chapter.

The next major advance was the gradual evolution of an elementary *memory* to assist the brain's processing of data. If past pleasures and pains were remembered this could provide additional motivation towards beneficial activities and away from harmful ones, to supplement the reaction provided by instinct, and a creature could actually improve its performance during its lifetime by learning from experience. No longer need it be pricked by a thorn before moving away, or search daily for its food, if it remembered the effects of thorns or where food had been found on previous occasions. At the same time the development of memory could allow good *habits* to form; activities which had proved enjoyable or beneficial in the past would then be indulged in without any specific motivation being necessary.

A development of great significance was the first glimmering of *reason*. When the ability to 'think things out' began to emerge, a new dimension was opened whereby a creature could actually predict the outcome of its actions, and by considering the probable results of several different courses it could choose that which promised the greatest satisfaction. In a certain sense the future as well as the past was now able to play a part in determining behaviour. We see here the beginnings of the 'will', enabling an animal to choose its actions deliberately in the light of the consequences. We see also the beginnings of conflict, for the brain may have strong reasons in favour of two or more courses of action, yet can choose only one, and must reject others despite their clamouring for satisfaction.

Moving forward in time to the early development of the human race itself, a great advance was made when man began to communicate through simple speech. No longer was the performance of each person determined solely by his own experience of the world; he was able to use the observations of all with whom he made contact. The survival value of such pieces of information as 'that plant is poisonous', or 'there is water over that hill' is obvious, and colonies in which speech was beginning to develop would soon succeed at the expense of those more backward. Here was evolution's final contribution to man's physical development.

As speech enabled knowledge to spread among the members of colonies, it would also allow the growth of what we now call *society*, groups of people actively co-operating, concerned not only with their own individual needs, but also the good of the whole community. This became possible only when we learnt to control some of our more selfish instincts. The most powerful instinct has always been that of self preservation, but even primitive animals often temper this with special care for their own offspring and near relations; some creatures which are normally timid can act ferociously if their young are threatened. We can easily see the survival value of this instinct, remembering that evolution is concerned not with the survival of individuals but of the species as a whole, and one's family members possess very similar genes to oneself. It therefore makes good sense to look after one's children and close relatives, and to show less tolerance to members of other families, whose genes differ significantly from one's own. However, societies can develop only when man learns to curb still further his natural tendencies; greater sympathy is now required in dealing with neighbours who are not close relatives, and a certain degree of altruism becomes an essential part of man's nature.

As we come nearer to our time, ever larger groups of people had to co-operate if they were to share successfully their resources and their knowledge, and the growth of *civilisation* can be seen as yet another example of the same evolutionary principle which has driven the development of life throughout its history. In such large groupings the elementary instincts of acquisition and procreation must often be suppressed. The practice of people 'owning' their own land and animals becomes essential, and we must temper our instinct of appropriating possessions with a respect for those of other people. The dangers of promiscuity are now so well known that few would query the survival value of monogamous relationships, both to reduce the spread of disease and to ensure stable households for the upbringing of children. It is easy, therefore, to explain why, as communities have grown in size, increasingly complex sets of laws and conventions have developed.

THE EVOLUTION OF MORALITY

Even this is not enough to ensure the smooth running of a community. It is possible to obey a country's laws to the letter, and yet to be thoroughly unkind or objectionable, and an unwelcome member of a civilized society. Legislation can make us more honest and less belligerent than we might otherwise be, but can do little to encourage the generosity, courtesy, reliability and truthfulness which makes civilisation possible. What is needed is a set of principles by which one can be guided in everyday dealings with neighbours, principles sufficiently general to cover the situations which a legal system cannot. If such principles are ingrained deeply in the mind then on most occasions they will be obeyed without effort as a matter of habit. Society can then run smoothly without relationships between members becoming stressful, and without individuals themselves being constantly harassed by the difficulty of making decisions. Such a set of conventions must rely for its continuity from generation to generation on the training we give to our children, and on the example we set them. Nor is this training restricted to the younger generation; it is not fashionable to lecture one's fellow men and women on their behaviour, but there is no doubt we continue to influence each other throughout life by our example, by our expressions of approval and disapproval, and by the attitudes we adopt to those we like and those we dislike.

Now all this has come about because of the pressures of natural selection. Communities which in the past have embraced a good set of laws and the right moral principles have flourished; their members have succeeded in sharing adequately the resources to keep them alive, they have not wasted their energy in petty feuds, and they have handed down to us the type of legal system and the ethical precepts which most countries now enjoy. This illustrates a completely new form of evolution, with a different medium for the transmission of characteristics from each generation to the next. The factors favourable to the survival of civilisation are not passed on biologically through a population's genes, but socially through training and example. We are not born with an in-built tendency to be honest, truthful and chaste; such characteristics must be inculcated through the influence of our elders. If sufficient time had been available, perhaps these qualities might have developed naturally through the normal evolutionary process; we would then have been born with an instinct for behaving in morally acceptable ways, and the parents and teachers of each generation would have been spared the duty of passing on the essentials of good behaviour to the next one. However, civilisation has grown up over a much shorter time-scale than that needed for ordinary evolutionary progress, and has become possible only because our ability to communicate has allowed this more rapid form of social evolution. The habits and precepts which must be taught to the members of each generation are far more vulnerable than if they were encapsulated in their genes; if a single generation fails in its duty to provide moral training for its young people then the standards of a society can fall back to a more primitive level within one person's lifetime. For civilisation to survive, each generation must bear in mind its heavy responsibility to pass on the essence of civilised behaviour to children who do not inherit biologically the characteristics which make life tolerable in today's sophisticated society.

OBJECTIONS TO THE CAUSAL EXPLANATION

How can this help support belief in a purely deterministic explanation of behaviour? The problems raised at the beginning of this chapter suggest three questions which must be answered if we are to advocate such a doctrine. (i) Why do people praise, blame, reward or punish one another, if their behaviour is determined by the rigid laws of cause and effect, and is not under their own control? (ii) Why do people often follow a good or generous course of action even when this is not in their own interest? (iii) What is the point in striving to succeed, if our behaviour, and so our ultimate success or failure, is not controlled by our own acts of will?

As we have shown, each generation's attempt to educate the next in the essentials of civilised behaviour has obvious survival value for societies such as ours. When we praise or blame our children we are helping prepare them to fit into society on their own merits, and perhaps we are vaguely aware of contributing something towards civilisation itself. We must not think that a deterministic explanation of behaviour renders such praise or blame ineffective; because our children and colleagues have the faculty of memory, the opinions we voice on their behaviour may remain in their mind, consciously or unconsciously, for many years, and provide one of the major factors determining their conduct throughout life. Our approbation or disapproval become elements in the causal chain which determines future action. Question (i) above is answered completely when we remember how fragile is civilisation, and acknowledge that its continuance depends entirely on the way people respond to each other's behaviour.

There are several agencies at work to explain the types of altruistic and self-denying behaviour which provided our second argument. The possibility of future praise or reward must not be overlooked, but there are undoubtedly cases in which this does not provide an explanation, where for example a person knows his good conduct is unobserved, or even that he is unlikely to survive to claim his reward. Some may believe their reward to await them in a future non-material life, but courage and generosity are not restricted to those with religious belief. There are two factors which can explain such conduct; if a person has been well disciplined in the types of behaviour approved of by society, good behaviour may have become strongly habitual, and will be practised without any conscious weighing of alternatives. Alternatively, if one's training has been more abstract and general, it may have laid down strong moral principles which, even if conscious deliberation is required when they are invoked, can still weigh more heavily in the decision-making process than considerations of personal gain or safety. The individual would claim to be obeying his conscience.

We can also answer the cynic who asks question (iii) above and says, 'Why should I try? If the future is pre-determined then it will be the same whether or not I make any effort.' This clearly is a false argument. The efforts we make all contribute to the causative chain which determines the future; it is not true to say that a world in which we do *not* try would have the same future as one in which we *do*. The fallacy lies in an implied belief that, in any given situation, we can either try or not as we choose. In fact the efforts we make are themselves determined by what went before, and we are mistaken in the belief that we could have done otherwise. It should not surprise us that we can make so fundamental a mistake in assessing the reasons behind our own behaviour; it is just another example of the mind's unwillingness to reveal its inner working. There is no reason why it should be otherwise; the mind's ability to comprehend the environment has great evolutionary value and explains why we are so successful in conquering it, but there is no comparable advantage in man understanding his own thought processes. Our evolution has not at all been hindered by our failure to understand the internal workings of the mind; confusion over the nature of time, the meaning of free-will or of moral responsibility has had no effect, for good or ill, on the physical development of the human race. Yes, we must continue to make an effort when we find things difficult, for this is an essential element in the process by which we accomplish the goals we set ourselves, but we should admit we are deceived if we believe we have any choice.

RESPECT FOR MORAL VALUES

The arguments of this chapter may be unpalatable to some readers who consider ethical principles too noble to be passed off as merely a feature of our evolutionary development. Moral values are being represented here as no more than a set of precepts invented by society to plug the gaps in our inherited instincts; they are not *absolute* in the sense that any other society elsewhere in the universe will have the same set, nor are they on a higher plane than the content of other aspects of education.

Arguments about the origins of morality, however, do not in any way lessen its importance. It cannot be maintained that the essentials of moral training are universal, for they clearly relate to the particular weaknesses in the human character which have been handed down to us. If a race of sheep were to develop an intellect like ours, and attempt to establish civilisations, their timidity would present a major hindrance; they would succeed only by making self assertion a highly praised quality. A race of ants, on the other hand, would need to teach each other that *individualism* is the highest moral virtue. The canons of correct behaviour which humans must pass on to each generation are those which happen to be missing from the instincts we inherit, and those needed to discourage the indiscriminate expression of those instincts. We must teach respect for other people's property only because of our strong acquisitive instinct; we teach that courtesy and generosity are owed to strangers only because our instinct is to confine these to members of our own family; we teach chastity because instinct encourages promiscuity. None of this lessens the respect we should feel for moral training in general; it is indeed our most important duty in the upbringing of the next generation.

SUMMARY

The meaning of *moral responsibility*, and the moral criteria by which behaviour should be judged, have exercised philosophers of all ages. Socrates (470-399 BC) believed that no-one committed evil knowingly, and so the secret of good behaviour was *knowledge*. For Aristotle (384-322 BC), each of the moral virtues was a mean between extremes; thus *courage* lies between cowardice and recklessness, and *generosity* between extravagance and meanness. The well known 'categorical imperative' of Immanuel Kant (1724-1804) involved a set of innate precepts, each of which must be obeyed absolutely, without reference to particular circumstances. J.S. Mill's *Utilitarianism* (1861) maintains that the right course of action is always that which promotes the greatest happiness.

No detailed examination of moral philosophy is attempted here, for the analysis of 'good' behaviour is outside the main argument of this book, but in this chapter we did need to examine the motivation lying behind good or altruistic conduct, and to justify the responsibility we attribute to others for their own behaviour, for at first sight these features appeared inconsistent with the philosophy we are advancing. A consideration of the way behaviour has developed since animals appeared on earth, and particularly since man began to form colonies demanding a high degree of co-operation, shows that this attribution of responsibility to others is an essential element in the passing on of our culture from one generation to the next, and in forming within each of us the belief that we behave altruistically because we so choose. Morality is seen to be no more than that body of doctrine needed to supplement our natural instincts, which are concerned primarily with our own selfish needs, so that our behaviour becomes acceptable in the complex society we now enjoy. The praise and blame, rewards and punishments we bestow on each other, represent the medium by which this doctrine is spread among the community, and passed on to future generations.

Chapter 7

CONSCIOUSNESS

BRAINS AND COMPUTERS

There is a remarkable similarity between the activity of a living creature and that of a computer. The brains of the higher animals are much more complex than any computer yet built, but the difference becomes narrower each year; it seems possible that someday we will be building control mechanisms for advanced robots which do not differ in principle from living brains.

The basic performance of any computer system can be analysed into three stages, *input, processing* and *output*. If a computer is handling the accounts of a mail-order company these three stages might consist respectively of the details on a customer's purchases, calculation of his updated balance, and his printed invoice; if it is controlling the operation of a chemical factory the stages will comprise messages from various sensors around the plant, working out the changes needed to keep the processes under control, and the signals sent back to the plant's pumps and heaters. The same three stages can be observed in the functioning of the human body and brain; our sense organs provide the input, the processing is represented by our thinking and decision making, and the output consists of the actions we perform.

The last two chapters attempted to show that even human behaviour, although complex, would be capable of explanation if ever we had all the necessary knowledge and understanding. The impression we have that somehow we can control our own actions in a way that overrides the input we receive from our sense organs was considered in detail in Chapter Five, and we concluded that this belief must be illusory. So are we left with a picture of the human mind that differs in principle from a computer only in being more complicated?

THE CERTAINTY OF CONSCIOUSNESS

There is something clearly missing from this picture. A computer is not *aware* that it is solving a problem; it does not reflect upon its own existence; it does not worry if a problem proves insoluble, nor does it feel pain when presented with inconsistent data or pleasure when it completes its task. Unless we can explain the source of human awareness, our picture of ourselves is not complete.

Consciousness can not be explained away in the same way that free will can, for there can be no doubt in your mind that you are conscious. Nor can you reasonably doubt that other people experience the same kind of consciousness as you yourself. You see others responding to their stimuli in much the same way that you respond; they seek those situations they enjoy in the same way that you do; they smile when their stimuli please them and they frown or protest when subject to unpleasant experiences. There is no way in which other people can *prove* to you that they are conscious, for their behaviour could be just a mechanical reaction to the stimuli they receive through their senses. A computer could easily be programmed to portray a face which smiles when presented with consistent data and scowls when its input is jumbled, to rebuke you in strong language when given a problem it cannot solve, or even to exclaim in an anguished voice, 'You are hurting me!', in response to certain combinations of input.

René Descartes (1596-1650) took the argument one stage further, and applied it not just to other people's consciousness, but to their very *existence*, and the existence of the whole of the rest of the universe. His famous exclamation '*Cogito: ergo sum*' (I think, therefore I am) was prompted by the certainty of his own existence, and a realisation that nothing else was quite so certain. The whole of his sensing and thinking might be no more

97

than a dream, so he could find no simple proof that the outside world really exists, but of his own existence there was no doubt, for *he* was doing the thinking. Descartes did, in fact, go on to demonstrate to his own satisfaction that the rest of the world does actually exist. His arguments here were much less cogent; but as was pointed out in an earlier chapter, a refusal to admit the reality of the material world presents many more problems than it solves. Most people accept the existence of the world because the doctrine is so much simpler than its converse.

In the same way we have no reason to doubt that other people are conscious; for knowing that you are conscious, and that others react in very similar ways to you when presented with similar stimuli, makes it much simpler to assume that all humans enjoy the same sort of awareness as you yourself. Indeed, *I* know the falsity of the belief that only *you* are conscious, for I know that *I* am. So although I could comprehend the behaviour of all living things, including humans, even if none of them (except myself) possessed consciousness, this would pose the compelling question of why all of you, without consciousness, behave in much the same way that I do, with it. People can describe to me what it feels like to be sad, happy, puzzled, or in pain, and their descriptions are so like those I myself would give of similar situations that I am convinced all humans have a consciousness very like my own.

HOW WIDESPREAD IS CONSCIOUSNESS?

But when we ask to what extent other creatures besides humans are conscious there is no such simple answer, for they are unable to describe their feelings to us, and we must rely solely on observing their behaviour. One can believe that even the highest animals, such as domestic pets, behave as they do without being aware of their own existence, and without experiencing pleasure and pain, but because in some respects their behaviour is quite like our own, most people will believe, very reasonably, that such creatures do enjoy the same sort of consciousness as we ourselves.

When we consider lower forms of life, people's beliefs differ more widely; and these beliefs can be assessed quite easily, for the degree of awareness we ascribe to any particular creature is correlated with the way we think that creature should be treated. Why do you try not to hurt or offend other people? The chief reason is surely the natural sympathy you have for your fellow men and women; you know what it feels like to be hurt or offended, and do not wish to inflict these feelings on others. In this way you are demonstrating your belief that they are conscious. So observing how people treat different types of living thing gives a good indication of the degree of consciousness they ascribe to them. Most of us are strongly affected if we see cruelty to a dog or a cat, but have we the same feeling regarding a fish, a worm, a fly, a plant, an amoeba, a microbe? The way we respond to the destruction or injuring of each of these beings provides a measure of how widespread we believe consciousness to be. And the differing attitudes people adopt towards sports such as hunting, fishing and shooting reveal irreconcilable differences in their attribution of consciousness to the creatures involved.

CONSCIOUSNESS AND THE BRAIN

Consciousness must be closely associated with the brain; nothing is more certain to cause a loss of consciousness than damage to the brain, or a drug which affects its operation. Some of the manifestations of consciousness, such as the perception of sights and sounds, the process of reasoning and the experiencing of pain, can actually now be related to specific physical changes within the brain, and can be observed with suitable equipment by physiologists. What we must consider is whether the conscious experience consists *solely* of the physical activity of the brain, or whether our consciousness is outside the realm of material things, and can never be explained in terms of neurons, electrical potentials and material particles because in some sense it observes the physical world from the *outside*.

If we accept the first possibility, that mental processes are no more than the activity of the physical brain, does this imply that artificial structures such as computers could ever be conscious in the sense that we are? The question is academic at present, for the most advanced computers are still several orders of magnitude less complicated than the human brain, both in their structure and in the data they handle. The day can be foreseen when computers will match the brain in scope and complexity, at least in their hardware. Will such machines experience anything resembling consciousness? Will they be able to reflect on their own existence? Will they enjoy some of the jobs they do and dislike others? Will they experience pleasure and pain? Will it be necessary to form a Society for the Prevention of Cruelty to Computers?

Let us consider the second possibility proposed above, that our consciousness is something non-physical which impinges on the brain at some point, that it is a characteristic essentially restricted to living creatures, and is outside the scope of the physicist or the physiologist. Many of us feel intuitively that there is something about the mind that transcends the limitations of base matter. A similar proposition was considered in Chapter Five in relation to the will, and was illustrated by Fig. 8, which shows a supernatural mind co-operating with the physical brain to control a person's decision-making processes. We presented arguments to oppose this suggestion in Chapter Five, but these cannot be applied here, for the mind we are now considering as the seat of our consciousness is just a passive observer of what goes on in the brain, and not an active participant in its functioning, as was the free-will we had to consider earlier. If we lie motionless with eyes closed, pondering the past day's events, planning tomorrow's activities, or trying to solve a problem, our mental processes seem far removed from the deterministic, uncreative world of physical science. Our imagination can fly away from the body to distant places and times, even to the furthest corner of the universe. We can hear the voices and see the faces of distant friends, we can compose letters or plan holidays, we can visualise the impossible. Surely all this cannot result just from the deterministic triggering of neurons in the brain.

Nevertheless we must remember the point made several times in previous chapters, that the closer we get to the centre of our thinking, the less reliable is our picture of what is there. We considered this when discovering how grossly incorrect is our perception of the nature of time. Now in considering the springs of our consciousness itself we are even closer to the heart of our thoughts, and intuition is still less to be trusted.

If we can successfully explain human consciousness without recourse to the non-physical we shall avoid many contradictions and perplexities. We can believe the human body and brain to be among the most complicated and potent structures in the whole universe and yet still maintain that they function within the laws of science. Gilbert Ryle wrote in 1950,

> most of us, correctly thinking that there are huge differences between a clock and a person, automatically but incorrectly explain these differences by postulating an extra set of ghost-works inside. We correctly say that people are not like clocks, since people meditate, calculate, and invent things; they get angry, feel depressed, scan the heavens, and have likes and dislikes. . . . Where we go wrong is in explaining these familiar actions and conditions as the operations of a secondary set of secret works.

The Physical Basis of Mind, ed. P. Laslett.

CONSCIOUSNESS AND COMPUTERS

So what are the principle features of this mysterious thing we call consciousness? We can easily distinguish a person who is conscious from one who is not because of an accident or an anaesthetic, and the difference between the two states should enable us to make a list of the chief factors which characterise consciousness. The most important are as follows:

(i) In the conscious state we respond to signals received from the sense organs. The unconscious person does not react to sense data.

(ii) When unconscious we do not perform any voluntary bodily movements.

(iii) An essential feature of the conscious state is the ability to recall past events in the memory. No such memories are active when we are unconscious.

(iv) Likewise, when unconscious we do not lay down memories of present events.

(v)   The various other types of thinking are denied us in the unconscious state; we do not have mental pictures, solve problems, or form judgements or intentions.

(vi)   We have no experience of pleasure or pain while unconscious.

(vii)   Lastly, when unconscious we experience no sentiments or emotions. We do not feel fear, elation, love or hate.

At least five of these aspects of consciousness are displayed by computer equipment in its present state of development. Computers respond to input from their keyboards and other devices in much the same way as we respond to stimulation of our sense organs. They control their output devices much as we can control the movements of our limbs. They possess memories to keep records of past events, and the results of present activity may be stored in memory for later recall, and the operation of their central processors as they perform lengthy calculations seems to compare with the activity of a brain as it attempts to solve problems.

In each case the process is much more involved (even if slower) in the human brain than in any present day man-made device. Consider firstly the manner in which we respond to sense data. The sense of touch is perhaps the simplest to understand, but shows a remarkable effect which is often overlooked. If something comes into contact with your left foot, say, then a message passes along the nervous system from the foot to the brain to make you aware of the contact. But you are unaware of the *message*; it appears to you that the foot itself senses the contact; in some way the brain *projects* the sensation back to the foot. Nothing like this happens in a computer; if several input devices are connected to one processor then some scheme must be provided to enable the processor to 'know' which of them is sending signals; it is aware of the fact that a device is about to send data *before* knowing which device.

The sense of sight is even more remarkable. The lens of the eye forms on the retina an image of the scene being viewed, and the optic nerve conveys data from the retina to the brain. However, it greatly surprises most people to learn that this image is upside-down. Every teacher of physics has experienced the disbelief of a class of students when first presented with this fact, but few such teachers will have succeeded in explaining that there should be no surprise; the students' reaction shows a failure to understand the relationship between the sense organ and the brain. There is not another internal eye in the brain viewing the retina, and having to invert its image. An even more perplexing aspect of seeing is revealed when we recall that, because the retina is two-dimensional, its images are in perspective. So when we look at a rectangular table the image is almost always an irregular quadrilateral, yet we immediately recognise the correct shape of the table top. It may be thought we had to learn in childhood how to interpret such perspective images as we gradually discovered how to make sense of the world about us, but if this were so, a young child would be able to draw in correct perspective as soon as it could handle a pencil. In fact a child is more likely to draw a table top as a true rectangle, and will have to be taught the rules of perspective when much older. If the interpretation of perspective images on the retina has been learnt, it has been learnt by mankind as part of his evolving intelligence rather than by individual children. An even greater puzzle is presented by the ease with which a young child can recognise a face, which it is seldom likely to see twice from the same angle or distance. How is this done? The more one considers it the more astonishing it seems. At the time of writing workers in the field of Artificial Intelligence are at last beginning to make some progress in the programming of computers to recognise such things as faces and signatures, and they may eventually devise reasonably reliable systems. Their method is to take advantage of the great speed of computers, which can complete hundreds of thousands of comparisons and calculations each second. The human brain certainly uses no such method.

Turning our attention now to human memory, one may think there is close resemblance with the memory characteristics displayed by computer equipment. The memories we lay down during our lives can be thought of as stored in RAM (Random Access Memory), while the tendencies with which we were born, presumably as a result of many generations of evolutionary development, correspond to the content of the computer's ROM (Read Only Memory). However, the similarity is only superficial; the working of the human memory being more sophisticated than that of any present-day computer equipment. In the first place, a computer remembers only what it is programmed to remember, while we appear to store a record of every event we experience. Our memories are stored at different levels, and the length of time a memory is retained depends upon the level. We can remember important happenings for a life-time, less important ones may be forgotten after a few weeks or days or minutes, while a telephone number we have just looked up is forgotten immediately we have dialled it. Again, the manner in which computers search their memories, making thousands of comparisons each second, is very different from the way we can recall facts, using an intricate system of association.

Another aspect of consciousness which may appear to mirror the activity of computing equipment is the process of passive thinking, such as problem solving. Watching a computer and a human playing each other at chess may give the impression that both go about it the same way, silently considering all possible moves before deciding which is the most appropriate. In principle this is true, although here again the computer relies more heavily on the speed with which it can follow through many thousands of possibilities, while the human can make use of experience in a much richer way. But many examples of human thought are more puzzling than this; computers do not visualise pictures, compose music, form moral judgements, or plan their own futures, and they certainly do not display curiosity about facts they want to know, or astonishment at those they do know.

CONSCIOUSNESS: FEATURES NOT DISPLAYED BY COMPUTERS

There are two aspects of consciousness which (certainly at present) have no parallel in the activity of computers. No-one today seriously believes such machines experience pleasure or pain, or that they can feel emotions such as love or fear. An attempt was made in an earlier chapter to show the evolutionary advantages of animals having a 'pain centre' that is triggered by

104

stimuli which are best avoided, and a 'pleasure centre' responding to those it is advantageous to continue. When the development of memory enabled past pleasures and pains to be recalled, the seeking or avoiding of such stimuli could play an even bigger part in determining behaviour. There will be no difficulty in building such tendencies into computer software if the tasks being undertaken make it worth while. When we build our first robotic domestic servants it may well be useful to include a 'pleasure centre' that is activated when they are praised, and a 'pain centre' triggered by a scolding. But this in itself will not ensure our robots actually *experience* pleasure or pain.

It may be thought that our feelings and emotions are even more difficult to explain in a purely physical description of the mind than our sense of pleasure and pain. If the mind is no more than a complicated machine, how can it possibly feel angry, afraid, or in love? Modern medicine associates with many of the emotions an emission into the bloodstream of one or more hormones from the endocrine glands which are found in various parts of the body. Those who maintain that the seat of the emotions is non-physical will say that these secretions merely *accompany* the emotions, and in some cases an actual purpose can be distinguished for the hormone. A discharge of adrenalin releases stores of sugar and increases the heart rate in readiness for fighting when an animal becomes enraged, but it can be argued that the discharge is not merely an accompaniment to the emotion, it *is* the emotion. If the body is able to sense the presence of a hormone in a way similar to that in which it detects contact with a hot or sharp object, then the emotions are no more difficult to explain than is our awareness of heat and cold, or the prick of a needle.

CONSCIOUSNESS: AN EXPLANATION

Although there are vast differences between today's computers and the human mind, it is possible that they are differences of degree and complexity rather than of principle. Most of the features of our consciousness are illustrated by modern digital equipment; perhaps it is only the wonderful richness of brain activity which raises its functioning above the threshold of self awareness. The way we deal with sense data and memories, and our capacity for such a wide range of unstructured and creative thinking are removed so far from the present-day activities of computers, that it should not surprise us if the difference raises our mental processes to a higher plane, and brings along with it those other features, such as the experiencing of feelings and emotions, which today's computers do not display.

Does this mean that some day in the future computers will indeed be sufficiently conscious to make it necessary to protect them from cruelty? If their hardware and software can ever approach the sophistication of the human brain, then they will indeed begin to demand the sort of respect we accord to conscious beings. Nevertheless although advances in technology during the past few years have shown the inadvisability of making negative predictions concerning its future progress, it does seem likely that man-made devices will never reach such a level. For how are we to imbue these machines with the ability to project their input data in the way that man's tactile and visual sensations are projected back to their source? How are we to simulate the marvellous refinement of the human memory? How are we to include among the factors determining our computer's responses not only all the memories it has accumulated throughout its life, but also the skills and instincts developed by previous generations of computer? How are we to extend its 'thinking' abilities to include visualisation of pictures, tunes and verses, understanding as well as knowledge, judgements of matters both factual and moral, and the capacity to contemplate the future and form long-term intentions? How can simple 'pleasure' and 'pain' centres be developed so as to respond not only to immediate and gross sense data, but also to the machine's own 'thoughts' and intentions, its concern for the future and its remorse for past errors? If our computer is also to experience emotions it will need components to mimic the action of man's glands, the hormones these secrete, and all the organs of the body which are influenced by them. We are surely on safe ground in claiming that this will never happen!

If we do ever want a computer to imitate an animal in a rage we shall find simpler ways of programming it to do so than building into it all the organs of an animal's body, simulating the secretion of adrenalin by some electronic suprarenal gland and expecting this to influence the electronic equivalent of its heart and lungs.

It is a mistake to think evolution has solved all its problems in the most effective way, and that we cannot sometimes improve on nature. We have found a more efficient way of travelling on land than using legs, and of travelling in the air than by flapping wings. If we wish to simulate human behaviour we shall certainly discover better ways than copying the human body in all its complexity, and then wondering whether we have created a structure with consciousness and emotions. There is no need yet to start collecting money for the protection of conscious computers from cruelty.

The human body and brain are so amazingly complex that we must not be surprised at finding their operation to be accompanied by an awareness and a consciousness, characteristics which may possibly be unique in the whole universe. Nor should we be tempted to seek a non-physical explanation just because we do not know where to look for a material one. Throughout history man has tried to excuse his ignorance by appealing to the supernatural; the rising and setting of the sun, the movements of the planets, and the fickleness of the weather were all ascribed to the whims of the gods before we could explain them otherwise; at a later date divine intervention was still necessary to explain the origin, diversity and functioning of living creatures. Now all these phenomena are known to fit quite well into a framework of scientific principles which are largely understood. The detailed working of the human brain still seems beyond the scope of science, but surely history should teach us not to abandon the search in favour of an appeal to the supernatural, or to claim that the proven methods of scientific investigation are unsuitable for exploring the brain's secrets. We need feel no shame if we are at present unable to comprehend fully the meaning of consciousness; there is no need to justify our incomplete understanding by postulating a non-material or ghostly element.

If there exists anywhere else in the Universe a mechanism as complicated as the human body and brain, able to handle as wide a range of data as we do, including signals from its senses, a complex memory system, a hormonal system to enable the inciting of sensations from within the body, and an ability to form mental pictures, to reason and to form judgements, then it seems certain such a machine will describe itself as being conscious. It might even believe itself to possess free will, unless its reasoning powers have convinced it that no meaningful definition can be found for such a term. If, on the other hand, the emergence of conscious life here is unique, then the earth must be a tiny oasis in a vast desert, an intriguing aberration in a system that was not meant to accommodate it. Nowhere else in the Universe, other than on earth, is there any evidence for the existence of conscious beings. In the unlikely event that we someday find intelligent creatures anywhere else in space, it will not follow that such organisms are necessarily conscious. In fact it is difficult to see what evolutionary advantage consciousness confers on a species; if humans could have developed all their physical and mental powers without it, there is no reason to doubt they would still have been as successful. Indeed the history of mankind might have been totally unaffected by the omission. Perhaps consciousness is just an accidental by-product of evolution, like the *appendix vermiformis*. But what a wonderful gift, demanding our eternal gratitude!

Chapter 8

MODERN PHYSICS

PHILOSOPHY AND MODERN SCIENCE

No longer can science and philosophy each plough its own furrow without any reference to the other. In previous centuries the two disciplines were essentially distinct; while science was concerned with the behaviour and interactions of material objects, philosophy was pursuing abstract ideas such as the mind, morality and truth, and the ultimate meaning of existence. Some of the great mathematicians and scientists of earlier centuries, such as Descartes and Leibnitz, did make significant contributions to philosophical thought, but generally the two branches of learning made little contact.

The advances made by science in the twentieth century have rendered this division of labour no longer feasible. Study of the mind has itself become a science, and the very basis of life is now treated as a branch of chemistry. Progress in cosmology is revealing an increasingly clear picture of the Universe and its history which must be relevant to any discussion of man's place within it. The two greatest developments in physical science this century have been the theory of relativity and quantum theory, and each of these impinges directly on our conceptions of space and time, of causality, and the meaning of reality itself.

Philosophers can now speak with authority only if they attempt to embrace the scientific developments bordering on the topics they discuss. No-one is entitled to express views on the meaning of life without some familiarity with molecular biology, or on the relationship of mind to body without some acquaintance with the physiology of the brain. It is now not acceptable for thinkers to declare views on the purpose or origin of the universe without reference to the knowledge amassed by twentieth century astronomy.

But the dialogue between philosophers and scientists must be two-directional. Some of the recent research in fundamental physics raises philosophical problems of such perplexity that many physicists are unwilling to wait for philosophy to absorb and analyse them, and are themselves attempting to devise their own interpretations. In recent years a number of those involved in sub-atomic research have published books explaining how their beliefs have been affected by the strange world they encounter in the laboratory. The philosophical frameworks which these scientists have advanced differ so widely that one is tempted to suggest they should perhaps have restricted themselves to their own field, and left the pursuit of ultimate meaning to others. This is not a fair comment, however, for the world of quantum mechanics is so strange and so contradictory that every thinking scientist working in that area must feel urged to search for a deeper understanding than that revealed by machines and calculators.

The proposals put forward by some of these physicists are indeed strange, and this book would not be complete without an attempt to appraise the more significant of them. This inevitably will involve discussion of scientific material at a deeper level than in the other chapters of the book, and so a brief outline will be offered here of the physical principles that must be taken into account.

We cannot, of course, present the teachings of relativity and quantum theory in detail; we can merely sketch some aspects of each theory in the hope of providing enough background for the arguments in the rest of the chapter to be understood, and readers who wish to study these concepts in greater depth can look elsewhere for a fuller explanation. There is no shortage of instruction on both topics at every level of difficulty, and several useful titles will be found in the bibliography at the end of the book.

RELATIVITY

The foundation of relativity theory is easy to understand; it is the fact that only *relative* motion can be detected, and that a state of absolute motionlessness is without meaning. When travelling by train you have no difficulty pouring out and drinking a cup of tea even if the train is moving at one hundred m.p.h. providing the track is straight and the train is not accelerating or braking. Even if you are aware of the train's motion, you are not likely to be thinking also of the motion of the countryside itself which moves at several hundred m.p.h. because of the earth's rotation, or the whole earth at many thousands of m.p.h. because of its motion around the sun. Galileo understood this in the early 1600s (but had to use a ship rather than a train in his explanation). When Newton published his Laws of Motion later in the seventeenth century they implicitly acknowledged that only relative motion has any significance. Then in the nineteenth century Maxwell, another brilliant scientist, explained the behaviour of light as completely as Newton had explained the motion of material bodies two centuries earlier; so successful was Maxwell's work that it led directly to the discovery of radio waves, and thus started a technological revolution familiar to everyone. It was soon realised, however, that Maxwell's equations *did* imply a significance for absolute motion, and several ingenious experiments were devised to find the real speed of the earth through space. All these failed; only relative motion could be detected, but no flaw could be found in Maxwell's theory; nature was presenting us with a contradiction. Several explanations were forthcoming, but it required the genius of Einstein to bring these ideas together in the Special Theory of Relativity in 1905. Some of the deductions from this theory appear difficult to believe, but Einstein realised there could be no alternative. Not only motion, but such concepts as *length, time* and *mass* also seemed to lose their reality. To give just one illustration, suppose two trains consist of equal numbers of identical carriages. One train is at rest (relative to the earth) and the other passes it at high speed. If an observer on the moving train measures the length of each he will find that the stationary train is shorter, but an observer on the stationary train would find that the moving train was shorter.

The only reason we are not usually aware of such discrepancies is that they are quite infinitesimal at the speeds trains travel. But if the relative speed of two objects is a significant fraction of the speed of light then the changes of length become substantial. Such speeds are encountered every day in experiments on sub-atomic particles in laboratories, and the results of these experiments invariably confirm that the Einstein contraction really exists.

It must be stressed that this effect is not simply due to the finite speed of light. Some people believe lightning always precedes thunder, but if you can persuade them to take into account the speeds at which sound and light travel you should be able to convince them that the two events actually occur together. Our two observers on the trains will still disagree over their lengths even after allowing for the time taken by light to reach their eyes from the ends of the trains.

Other predictions of the theory of relativity which are repeatedly confirmed in laboratories are an increase in the mass of an object when moving at high speed, and the fact that no two material bodies can ever have a relative velocity greater than that of light.

The most significant prediction from our point of view, however, concerns the nature of time, which is also found to depend upon an observer's state of motion. No meaning can be attached to a statement that two events are *simultaneous*. If two observers are moving relative to each other there are situations in which one of them might describe two distant events, A and B, as simultaneous, while the other would consider A to occur before B. (Again it must be stressed that the discrepancy would remain after due allowance had been made for the time taken for light to reach the observers from each event.) This effect is best illustrated by means of a space-time diagram like those developed in Chapter Three, and the reader is asked to refer back to Fig. 1. It will be remembered that if you are moving (relative to me, for I have drawn the diagram) your world-line does not lie straight up and down, but at an angle depending on your speed. Now Einstein teaches us that not only is your world-line at an angle, but the horizontal line which represents all those events which you consider simultaneous is also at an angle; Fig. 1. has actually been drawn wrongly. An analogy from the

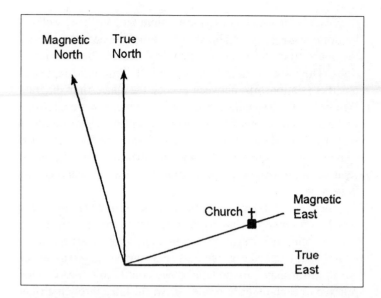

Fig 10. Using Magnetic Bearings, the church is due East, but using
True Bearings its direction has a Northerly component.

world of orienteering should be easy to understand. If you are
using a compass to find your way across a moor you may see a
distant church due East. But you need to check whether your
compass indicates *true* bearings or *magnetic* bearings. If the
North mark on your compass indicates magnetic north, while
your colleague's indicates true north, then he will find the church's
direction to have a small northerly component (Fig. 10). The
further away is the church, the further north of your colleague's
West-East line will the church appear to lie. Not only the North-
South line of your compass, but also the East-West line lie in a
different direction from your colleague's, and some of the church's
Eastward distance has been converted into Northward distance.
Something similar happens to a space-time diagram if you are
moving in relation to me; because of the motion, your world line
is turned through an angle from the vertical as Fig. 1. shows, but
in addition, the horizontal line representing those events you
consider to be occurring 'now' is also turned. So an event which
appears to me to occur 'now' (because it lies on my 'now' line)
may appear to you to occur at some different time (because it
does not lie on your 'now' line).

113

Two events which I describe as 'simultaneous' may well not be simultaneous to you. This result is important because it shows the space-time diagrams we drew in Chapter Three in a new light. They are no longer mathematical fictions to represent abstract relationships between events; the space-time diagram is more like the way things really are than our conventional spatial picture which we think of as changing as time flows along its way. Einstein shows us that space and time are essentially the same thing, and our diagrams indicate that under conditions of relative motion a certain proportion of *my space* can become *your time*.

There are places on the surface of the earth where magnetic North is as much as ninety degrees from true North. If my compass measures magnetic bearings and yours true bearings, a church that I describe as due East could appear to you to be due North. So it may be wondered if we could move fast enough relative to each other to rotate our world-lines through a right angle; it would be exciting if we could turn the whole of a distance into a time, and a time into a distance! But we must remember that nothing can travel faster than light. The angle that this represents on the space-time diagram depends on the two scales we take for distance and time; it is often convenient to choose these scales so that the world-line of a light ray lies at forty five degrees to the vertical axis, and the maximum angle through which our diagram can rotate is then forty five degrees; we cannot turn space completely into time, nor time into space.

(It must be admitted that a major simplification was made in writing the previous two paragraphs. In fact the mathematics of Einstein's four-dimensional space-time differs from that of a two-dimensional moor in such a way that if your imaginary North-line (i.e. your world-line) is turned clockwise, then your East-line (i.e. your 'now' line) turns anti-clockwise; the two lines do not remain at right angles. This means that our drawing of the compass bearings on the moor cannot really be taken to represent the situation described in space-time. Still the gist of the argument is not altered by this, and the theory of relativity does show that space and time are linked inextricably.)

The scientific deductions from Einstein's theory are extensive and profound. The philosophical deductions are perhaps less significant, but the new insight it gives into the relationship between space and time provides further evidence that our perception of time as something which flows or moves is false. We must allow space-time diagrams to play a bigger part in our thinking, for their portrayal of the way events are related in four dimensions is closer to reality than the more usual view we take in which time has a different nature from distance, and is endowed with the artificial property of change or motion.

QUANTUM THEORY

If the influence of relativity on philosophical thought is not profound, the same cannot be said of quantum theory, some of whose teachings suggest that we may now need to reconsider the meaning of reality, the position of mankind in the world, and the significance of consciousness. By the end of the nineteenth century it was thought that the nature of light was largely understood, apart from the uncertainty mentioned above. Light was known to consist of waves, something like the sound waves which travel in air to give us the sensation of hearing, but in the case of light consisting of varying electrical and magnetic fields travelling through empty space. Their velocity was known accurately, as were the wavelengths and frequencies of lights of different colours, and many phenomena were explained completely by this knowledge. A few anomalies remained. One of these concerned the distribution of wavelengths radiated by a hot body such as red-hot metal or the sun. The wave theory seemed to indicate that it should radiate equally at all frequencies, whatever the temperature; the colour of the light emitted by a hot body should not depend upon its temperature, and the dull glow from an electric fire should be the same colour as the molten steel in a furnace. In order to resolve this difficulty Max Planck (1858-1947) made the apparently innocent suggestion that light energy was emitted in tiny discrete packets, which he called *quanta* (the plural of *quantum*). Before long it was realised that many of the other problems associated with the transmission of light could also be resolved if these quanta were treated, in fact, as *particles* of light, (later christened 'photons'). The wave theory was quietly forgotten when discussing some types of experiment, and the photons forgotten when others were performed. But the two ideas seemed quite incompatible, and no-one could explain why light behaved like waves 'on some days of the week', and like particles on others.

To make matters worse, it was also found that particles of matter, such as the electrons which form part of every atom, behaved sometimes as if they were also waves, whose wavelengths could be measured, and which could spread out to fill the whole of an open space just like waves of light. When attempts were made to measure the position and speed of an atomic particle it was found impossible ever to measure both accurately at the same time. At first this was attributed simply to the clumsiness of the experiments. To see where a particle is, one must shine a light on it; the smallest amount of light was one photon, and this gives the particle a knock sufficiently powerful to alter the speed one is trying to measure also. It transpires that the more accurately we wish to measure the position, the more energetic must be the light quanta, and the less accurately can we estimate the speed. More cunning methods were then tried, such as passing a beam of particles through a small hole in a screen. If a particle gets through the hole we then know its position without bombarding it with light quanta. But nature again confounds us, for the particles are found to spread out after going through the hole, and the smaller the hole, the wider the angle of spread, meaning that the direction of the particles' motion cannot be accurately known. This discovery is an example of a much more general phenomenon which was discovered by Werner Heisenberg (1901-1976), the 'Uncertainty Principle' which was mentioned in a previous chapter.

One of the simplest experiments to demonstrate the wave nature of light was devised by Thomas Young in 1801 and is illustrated in Fig. 11. A is a source which produces light of one particular wavelength, B and C are two small holes in an opaque screen, and light which gets through then shines on another screen at D. If only one hole is open, the light spreads out as described in the previous paragraph and illuminates the central area of D more or less uniformly, but if both holes are open, a pattern of

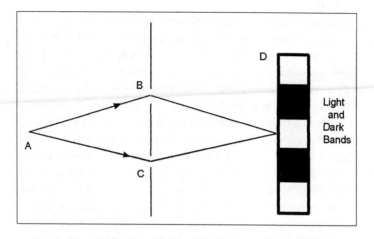

Fig. 11. When a monochrome light source, A, illuminates a screen, D, through two small holes, B and C, alternate light and dark bands are produced.

dark and light bands is produced. This is easily explained by the wave theory of light, because in some places the waves from the two holes are 'in phase' and so reinforce each other, while in others they are out of phase and can cancel completely. But suppose we replace the screen D with an array of light detectors sufficiently sensitive to detect each individual photon, and reduce the brightness of the light source so that the photons arrive one by one. What do we observe now? Each individual photon can arrive at only one point on the screen, and will trigger only one of the detectors; but more of them arrive at the places where the bright bands of light were observed than in the dark bands. A fact which was easy to explain when light is regarded as waves is very puzzling when it is thought of as particles. Through which hole are the photons passing? How do they know where the other hole is? In an attempt to find out what is happening let us now close one of the two holes. The photons are then found to arrive uniformly again over the whole screen; the light and dark bands have vanished.

This last fact is so strange that it deserves a paragraph to itself. By *closing* one of the holes through which the photons are passing we can *increase* the number arriving at some parts of the screen. The formation of the bands, so easy to explain in terms of the wave theory of light, becomes inexplicable

117

when we consider the light to consist of individual particles.

The pattern of light and dark bands, and the fact that they are still produced even if the photons arrive singly, shows that we must regard the light as waves of *probability*. We cannot know where any particular photon will strike the screen, but it is more likely to arrive in a bright band than a dark one. If you see a stranger in a train you may have no idea where he lives, but he is more likely to live in London than in the Highlands of Scotland because not many people live in the Highlands of Scotland. But the paradox remains; if the photon passes through the upper of the two holes it must avoid the dark areas only if the lower hole is also open; how can the hole through which it does *not* pass affect its motion?

The results of this experiment are perplexing for another reason which was touched upon in Chapter Five. If the point of arrival of the photon is dependent on probability, this must mean it is not governed by laws of cause and effect. It seems no longer to be true that identical experiments yield identical results; the fundamental particles of matter and energy appear not to behave deterministically. However, the world of familiar experience is built up from these particles, and everything we find happening around us is ultimately due to the way they behave; how can our everyday world appear to be deterministic, if it is composed of particles whose behaviour is not? Of course probability plays a part in many everyday experiences, as with the toss of a coin or the fall of a dice, and we do not think of these events as being undetermined; we simply lack the knowledge and ability to predict them. Some physicists consider that the unpredictability of the photon depends in a similar way on a system of 'hidden variables' which we have not yet discovered, but others believe the randomness to be intrinsic, and not merely the result of our incomplete knowledge.

Despite these mysteries, quantum mechanics has become one of the most successful theories of all time. It has explained the structure of atoms and the details of the light they emit in laboratories and stars; it has explained radioactivity, the whole of chemistry and important aspects of molecular biology. It has led to the discovery of the laser and the transistor on which all modern electronics depend. Every day its predictions are confirmed in the experiments performed with particle accelerators in various parts of the world, the numerical accuracy of these predictions being quite unprecedented. Central to the calculating power of this theory is a concept called the *wave function*, which is usually written down as the Greek letter *psi*, and which represents indirectly the probability function we have described. Just as a population map of Great Britain can indicate the probability that a person of unknown address lives in a particular area, so the wave function may indicate the probability of an electron, say, being found at different positions in space. In fact *psi* is a little more complicated than this, and *two* numbers are required to specify its value at any point, for which the mathematician often uses one *complex number*. For the benefit of those who understand complex numbers the following explanation is framed so that it does describe, as far as possible, how the complex number *psi* behaves in some of the simpler experiments conducted by particle physicists; but for those whose mathematical knowledge does not embrace complex numbers, let us pretend that *psi* is simply an ordinary number which may lie between the values of -1 and +1 inclusive. It should be clear that *psi* cannot directly represent a probability, for probability values must lie between 0 and 1. The probability of a coin falling 'heads' is 1/2, or a dice showing a '1' is 1/6. If an event is *impossible*, such as a dice showing a '7', then its probability is 0, and if it is *certain*, such as a coin falling 'either head or tail' then its probability is 1. Now the rule which the quantum scientists use for converting values of *psi* into probabilities is not difficult to apply, and is as follows: take the modulus of *psi*, which we write as $|psi|$, (and which in our simplified description means ignoring the minus sign if there is one), and square it, giving $|psi|^2$. Thus if *psi* is 1/2 the corresponding probability is 1/4, and if *psi* is -1/2 the probability is again 1/4; in each case the *psi* value corresponds to a probability of one quarter.

There are two simple rules which apply to the probabilities of compound events, and which we must learn if we are to understand how to manipulate *psi* correctly. Firstly, if an event can happen in two or more alternative ways, then we *add* the probabilities of the alternatives to find the overall probability of the event. As an example, the probability of a dice showing 'an even number' is clearly 1/2, and of its showing '1' is 1/6, so the overall probability of its showing 'either an even number or a 1' must be 1/2 + 1/6, which comes to 2/3. The second rule applies when an event involves two or more sub-events *all* of which must occur, and then we *multiply* the probabilities of the sub-events to find the final probability of the whole event. So if we toss a coin and roll a dice at the same time, the probability of scoring 'a head and a 1' must be 1/2 × 1/6, which comes to 1/12.

Exactly the same rules apply to *psi* as to probabilities. If *psi*$_1$ is the *psi* value for our light quantum to go through the top hole and reach a certain point on the screen, and *psi*$_2$ the value for the bottom hole, then the overall *psi* value is *psi*$_1$ + *psi*$_2$, and the corresponding probability is found by squaring the modulus of this quantity. But the rules state that you must add the *psi* values first and then square, and not vice versa. Probabilities are always positive, and so adding probabilities together always increases them, but *psi* may be negative. Indeed if the two *psi* values are equal and opposite they will add to give 0, which then squares to give zero probability. This shows how there can be points on the screen which receive no photons; the two wave forms we have added are said to interfere with each other, and the resulting picture on the screen is called an *interference pattern*. It is this strange behaviour of the wave-function which is at the root of the contradictions presented by Quantum Mechanics.

Let us return to the two-holes experiment, but instead of light let us use a beam of electrons. As we have seen, these can behave as waves rather than particles, and if we arrange for them all to have the same speed, and so the same wavelength, their points of arrival on the screen will again form an interference pattern, with bands of high and low density. Whichever hole an electron goes through it must in some manner 'know' whether the other one is open, (unless in some way it goes through *both* holes), for only then can it 'know' which areas of the screen are to be densely populated and which sparsely. It would be fun to know whether an electron can in fact go through both holes, so let us place a detector close to each to see if the electron passes that way. These detectors could work either by shining a light across the holes and looking for flashes, or by using a sensitive electrostatic instrument to detect the electron's electric charge. We shall then find that indeed some go through one hole and some through the other; if the electrons are fired one by one only one detector will register each time. So the particles seem *not* to go through both holes at once. But wait! We forgot to look at the screen. After installing our electron detectors the interference pattern on the screen has vanished; shining a light on the particles has destroyed the distribution we were investigating, and they are once again scattered uniformly over the screen. So we still do not know whether an electron must pass through both holes when the interference pattern is being produced. Nature's magic has defeated us, and she will not reveal how she does the interference trick.

This experiment, and the one in which we attempt to measure position and speed simultaneously, seem to indicate that the act of measurement or observation has a special significance in nature. When we observe the position of a particle by some means or other, the *psi* wave which until then indicated the probability of its occupying different positions appears suddenly to collapse. This sudden change, arising only when we ourselves probe into an experiment, has been responsible for much dispute between physicists, and half a century of argument seems to have brought agreement no nearer.

Some have maintained that only the intervention of a conscious being can bring about this collapse. Many experiments have been done in attempts to prove or disprove this thesis, and many more 'thought experiments' have been proposed which for some reason are not suitable for actual execution, but which might throw light on the problem merely by being considered. Perhaps the most famous of these has become known as 'Schrödinger's cat'. A situation is envisaged involving a radio-active nucleus which has a 50% probability of disintegrating during the next hour. This is put into an opaque box containing an unfortunate cat, and a piece of machinery which will smash a flask of poisonous fluid if the nucleus does actually disintegrate, the fumes from the fluid being sufficient to kill the cat immediately. Now until the box is finally opened no-one can know whether the cat is alive or dead, and if it requires the knowledge of an intelligent conscious individual to collapse the waveform describing the radio-active nucleus and everything else in the box, then it can be true to say neither 'the cat is dead' nor 'the cat is alive' until after the box is opened. Some scientists have maintained that the animal must in some way have been both dead and alive during this period; others have found the paradox so overwhelming that they deny any meaning can be attached to the existence of the cat, or anything else, unless it is actually observed, echoing the philosophy of Bishop George Berkeley who proposed in the eighteenth century that nothing exists except while someone is watching it.

Throughout his life, Einstein refused to accept any element of 'unreality' in the material world, nor was he prepared to believe the random factor in quantum behaviour represented anything more than our own ignorance of the rules by which it was really governed. He expressed this, somewhat allegorically, in his famous remark that 'God does not play dice'. In both these beliefs he was in conflict with Niels Bohr (1885-1962), one of the chief architects of quantum theory and chief spokesman for those who believed that much we observe in the world has no real existence except when an observation 'collapses' the wave. The discussion between the two great men continued from about 1927 until Einstein's death in 1955, and while it remained good natured it caused both men much thought and worry. One of the cleverest thought experiments was devised in 1935, and is known as the EPR experiment, after the names of Einstein, Podolsky and Rosen who designed it. It involved the creation of two identical particles which fly off in opposite directions, generated in such a way that they must necessarily have the same speed. Now quantum theory denies the possibility of knowing simultaneously the position and speed of a particle, but what is to stop us measuring the position of one and the speed of the other? Einstein showed that, however far apart the two particles had moved, the measurement we make on one of them must immediately affect the probabilities involved in measurements of the other. As this could imply the transmission of an influence faster than light, Einstein maintained that it proved something was wrong with quantum theory. Bohr, on the other hand, insisted that such an influence *could* be transmitted instantaneously, but that even though it did travel faster than light, the Theory of Relativity was not infringed. The influence did not involve a material particle, nor was it capable of carrying any information, for the randomness in the behaviour of both particles would ensure that an observer of one still did not know what sort of observation had been made on the other. Since 1935 there have been such improvements in technology and experimental methods that it is now possible to conduct experiments like the one Einstein and his colleagues proposed. In its original form the EPR test is not quite suitable for performing in the laboratory, but several equivalent experiments have now been done, culminating in one by Alain Aspect in Paris in 1982. These have shown conclusively that the predictions of quantum mechanics are confirmed, and Einstein was wrong. We are forced to abandon the belief that an event can influence directly only those events which are nearby; such influences can indeed propagate at speeds greater than that of light.

PHILOSOPHY OF THE QUANTUM PHYSICISTS

In the face of these perplexities many physicists and mathematicians now feel compelled to venture into the realms of philosophy. The books written in recent years describing the history of Quantum Mechanics and attempting to offer an underlying philosophy present a wide range of solutions.

As mentioned above, Niels Bohr thought it necessary to question the reality of much that we had taken for granted in the material universe, maintaining that only when a wave-form 'collapsed' could we say anything of significance about the world. He was not one of those who insisted that this collapse required the awareness of a conscious mind, but that any 'irreversible act of amplification' would be sufficient. This seems to imply that he would not insist on Schrödinger's cat spending some time both dead and alive, for the destruction of the flask of poison would certainly count as an irreversible amplification of the radioactive decay of the atom. But the point at which the wave-form collapses remains poorly defined, and another school of thought is represented by Eugene Wigner who believes that *mind* is a completely different entity from *matter*, and that the collapse occurs only when knowledge of an event enters a conscious and intelligent mind. Because mind is so clearly defined, this is an event involving no ambiguity. According to Wigner the cat must be in a state of suspended animation, neither dead nor alive, until the box is opened.

A much more startling proposal was made by Hugh Everett in 1957, and has been accepted by a number of subsequent writers. Everett evades the problem of the collapsing wave-form by saying that it never happens; whenever there is a choice at the quantum level between two possible events then *both* happen, and the result is *two whole universes*, identical except that in one the first choice was made and in the other, the second. So there is one universe in which Schrödinger's cat is dead and one in which it is alive; the number of universes is constantly doubling. Each time a division occurs two copies of *you* will be generated, each enshrining your personality and all your old memories and its own continuation of your consciousness, but with no possibility of communication between the two copies. The many copies of *you* will then go on to live different lives.

Other writers have approached the problem of human consciousness in other ways. While Roger Penrose does not believe the working of the mind to be essentially different from other material processes, he describes in detail a type of deterministic behaviour which he calls 'non-algorithmic' and which in consequence is incapable of being predicted; he maintains that this leaves some scope for the operation of free-will. Danah Zohar, on the other hand, believes that consciousness is universal; even an electron has it in some rudimentary form.

AN ALTERNATIVE VIEW

It is astonishing that scientists have talked themselves into such unlikely positions as these. The root of the trouble is that, although we know the quantum world to be so different from the world of common experience, we are unable or unwilling to discard the prejudices developed from familiarity with the world as we normally observe it. When we think of an atomic particle having collisions with other particles we bring to mind a picture of snooker balls colliding on a billiard-table; at each moment of time we can see the balls moving over the table, and can picture their whole trajectory as continuous lines, and imagine their position and speed at each point of their path; so we imagine the same must apply to an electron between any two consecutive collisions, and we are perplexed if its trajectory seems to have an element of unreality. Then again, we know that in everyday life bodies influence each other only in their immediate vicinity, or by sending out signals which we can picture travelling through space, so we refuse to believe fundamental particles can influence each other over great distances or times without any signal passing which we can visualise.

Our greatest handicap is, once again, the jaundiced view we have of time, because of our knowledge of the past but not of the future, giving us the false belief that there is one particular moment of time which we call 'now', and that this moment is moving. One result of this is the intense interest we take in whether the future history of the Universe is determined by the past, a question that in itself is no more important than whether the whole past of the Universe could be calculated from a knowledge of the future (or whether knowing the history of the part of the Universe lying to the North of the plane of the earth's orbit would enable us to work out the history of the other half). We find it surprising that we cannot determine by calculation the future behaviour of a system of atomic particles from our knowledge of the past, and believe this indicates an uncertainty in future events *themselves* rather than just in our knowledge of them. If the idea of 'now' is purely subjective, however, and has no parallel in the outside world, then there is no real dividing line to separate past and future; the distinction must be false, and there can be no essential difference between the two regions into which we think time is divided.

One physicist who remained aloof from the more extreme speculations of his fellows was Richard Feynman (1918-1988). He is acknowledged as one of the greatest thinkers of the century, and he also excelled in communicating his ideas to those with lesser intellect than himself, often in an amusing and

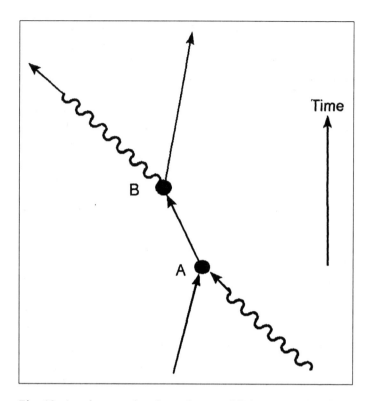

Fig. 12. An electron absorbs a photon of light at A and emits an identical photon a moment later at B.

individualistic way. Feynman realised that the influences of particles on each other were best illustrated on a space-time diagram rather than on one showing only the dimensions of space. Fig.12 is a typical example, in which an electron (whose world-line is represented by straight lines) absorbs a photon of light at A (the photon's world-line being shown as a wavy line), and after a short time re-emits it at B. He developed a theory for explaining many of the phenomena of Quantum Mechanics without needing the difficult mathematical relationships devised by Erwin Schrödinger (1887-1961), and dismissed as unnecessary such ideas as the 'uncertainty principle' and the 'collapse of the wave-packet'.

If we are to understand how Feynman's principles can dissolve many of the apparent paradoxes of the quantum world, it must be realised firstly that a particle can have no effect on anything else unless it *collides with, emits* or *absorbs* another particle, engaging in what Feynman calls a 'coupling'. A photon can affect the retina of your eye, or a photographic plate, only if it strikes it and collides with an electron there; an electron can be observed only if it emits a photon; two electrons can repel each other only if photons of electric force travel between them, and the gravitational attraction between pairs of particles is believed also to result from the emission and absorption of 'gravitons'. It follows from this that we can know nothing at all about the behaviour of a particle between one coupling and the next. If an electron had a coupling at A a moment ago and now has one at B we can know nothing of its behaviour in between these two moments; we certainly have no reason to believe it has travelled from A to B in a straight line at constant speed, as Fig.12 seems to show.

I want to pursue this argument a little further than Feynman, and suggest that we have no reason to assume the electron ever travelled *at all* from A to B, nor even that it *existed* between the moment it was at A and the moment it is at B. The type of space-time diagram developed by Feynman to represent the interactions of particles, such as Fig.12, remains a good picture, but its accuracy can be improved if we omit from it the straight and wavy lines which indicate the trajectory of each particle between each of its couplings and the next (Fig.13).

This does not imply that the couplings are unrelated; indeed the rules relating couplings to each other embrace the whole of physical law. The conservation of electrical charge and mass ensure that under many situations particles can be treated as if each does in fact have a continuous existence, as Feynman's diagrams suggest. The lines on these diagrams must not be taken to represent journeys from one coupling to another, but they do indicate *which* particles are involved in particular couplings. Furthermore, the well known physical laws of conservation of momentum and energy restrict the relative positions of adjacent couplings, as does the rule forbidding particles to travel at speeds greater than that of light; Feynman's lines may not represent trajectories, but they do remind us that a certain amount of information must be passed from each coupling to its neighbours. It can be argued that when we understand completely all the

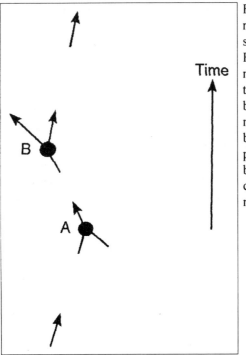

Time

B

A

Fig. 13. This represents the same process as Fig. 12, but the middle of each track is omitted because we have no reason to believe either particle exists between one coupling and the next.

rules relating couplings, then the task of physics will be completed.

The second trap we must avoid is of being surprised by the random element in the relationships between couplings. Causation in the familiar world of experience means that we can calculate the occurrence of some events if we know of the occurrence of others. In particular, we can sometimes predict the future behaviour of a system if we know its present state, and in cases too complex to allow prediction, we know that identical situations existing now will lead to identical future behaviour. The connections between the couplings of atomic particles are *not* causal in this sense, as they involve an essential element of probability, of genuine randomness. If they were indeed causal, then of course this would explain why we find strict determinism in the more familiar world of everyday experience. But the converse argument is false; knowing that the macroscopic world behaves deterministically does not imply the same must be true at the atomic level. If the particle rules are statistical rather than deterministic this leads just as certainly to causal laws in the world of common experience, for the number of particles involved in any event which we can observe is so great that it can be explained equally well whether the rules relating couplings are probabilistic or deterministic.

Nor must we be alarmed to discover that these relationships are non-local, and can involve instantaneous propagation through space. We know relativity teaches that neither particles nor information can travel faster than light, but this restriction is manifest only by the couplings themselves. There is no reason to suppose any such rule governs the *probabilities* involved in remote couplings. The EPR experiments do illustrate a situation in which couplings at separate points have an instantaneous effect on each other's probability, but in such a way that no information can be transmitted at super-luminal speeds. Consideration of Young's experiment described earlier suggests that here also the influence between couplings can 'feel out' the layout of the whole experiment instantaneously, and in some sense is 'aware' of the fact that two holes are open in the screen between the emitted particle and its point of detection. Indeed, the denial by relativity of any precise meaning for the term 'simultaneous' implies that we must be ready on occasions to see influences acting backwards in time. Not only must we regard the whole of space as open to scrutiny by the rules directing quantum behaviour, but they must have access to the whole of space-time in pursuing their task of connecting couplings with each other. Our everyday experience is derived from the behaviour of large numbers of particles, and even in laboratory experiments particle physicists can only observe couplings; the rules relating such couplings must be discovered indirectly.

In many experiments these rules are encapsulated in a remarkable mathematical formula known as Schrödinger's equation, which describes how the appropriate wave function, i.e. the distribution of *psi* values, develops as we imagine time to progress. The error that appears to have been made by many physicists is in supposing that *psi* allows us to calculate the probability distribution for the positions of particles *between* one coupling and the next, whereas in fact it can refer only to the possible positions of the *next* coupling. The argument being advanced here maintains that a particle *does not exist* between one coupling and another, and so *psi* cannot have anything to do with the position it occupies during this time.

There is another respect in which the wave function has been misunderstood. *Psi* clearly has something to do with nature's rules governing the relationships between couplings, for *psi* is used to calculate their probable positions. But it also relates to the state of our *knowledge* of these couplings, and it is this dual significance which has proved so perplexing. Let us take a simple example. Suppose a point A on the space-time diagram represents a coupling involving a photon, and B shows the place and time of a possible position for its next coupling. There will be a value of *psi* from which we can calculate the probability that 'if A represents one coupling and B represents the *time* of the next coupling, then B also shows its *position*'. Now suppose we could be aware of the situation at a moment in time *between* the occurrence of A and B. Because A is in the past we could *know* that it has occurred — there might be a record of A having happened, either on some recording machine or in our memory. There can be no record of B at that time because the Second Law of Thermodynamics forbids the recording of future events, as explained in Chapter Four. So how does the situation appear to us at this moment of time between A and B? We know the photon is moving with the speed of light, but not its direction of motion, so we cannot say where its next coupling will occur, but if it happens to be 'now' we have a good idea how far it will be from A. So if we calculate the value of $|psi|^2$ at different points in space, those points where its value is greatest lie on a spherical shell around A. As time progresses the radius of this shell will increase; we say that the wave representing the photon is being radiated from A. But this is 'all in the mind'. There is no wave; *psi* is simply an artefact to help our calculations. The picture we have of *psi* distributed through space, and representing a wave radiating outwards from A, owes its form solely to the artificial position we are in, of knowing about A but not about B.

We should have realised something was wrong with our picture from the very fact that our spherical shell is expanding. The laws of quantum mechanics are reversible with respect to time. The relationship between the events A and B in space-time is symmetrical; which of the points comes first in time makes no difference, and this is certainly not true for our spherical wave. If time were reversed we would have a wave converging on A from all directions, and finally vanishing from sight at the moment A occurs. Nothing like this ever happens. Physicists call expanding waves 'retarded', and waves contracting to a point 'advanced', and have long wondered why the latter never occur. (There are, of course, situations in which a body emits many photons, and can *then* be thought of as radiating light outwards, but this occurs only if the body is hotter than its surroundings, and we have a problem for Thermodynamics rather than for atomic physics. We know that when a system is not in thermal equilibrium its development is not reversible.)

What happens then if we continue watching until event B actually occurs? Another irreversible thing happens, the wave-form 'collapses'. Of course it does! A moment ago we knew only a relationship between the time the photon has been travelling and its distance from A; but now we actually know the time and place of B. Our knowledge changes instantaneously, and with it the form of our *psi* distribution. The location of B no longer involves probabilities. Similar situations happen to us every day: suppose I draw a card from a pack and ask you to guess it. You might say 'The Queen of Spades', and the probability that you are right would be 1/52. But suppose you catch a glimpse of the card and see that it bears a picture; the probability then becomes 1/12. Finally, when I show you the card, the 'wave-form collapses'! If it actually *is* the Queen of Spades the probability becomes 1, and if not it becomes 0. Probabilities by their nature are dependent on the state of our knowledge, and so are the *psi* distributions used by particle physicists.

THE QUANTUM PARADOXES

Let us take as a basis for understanding the significance of Quantum Mechanics the following three principles. (i) The only things which really exist in the world are couplings between particles. (ii) The relationships between adjacent couplings are restricted by laws such as the conservation of energy and the forbidding of speeds greater than that of light; there remains an element of uncertainty which is governed by statistical laws. (iii) The laws themselves may act instantaneously throughout the whole of space-time. These ideas should be sufficient to explain all the puzzling phenomena which Quantum Theory describes.

The wave-particle duality of both light and matter follows immediately from the nature of the laws themselves, for Schrödinger's equation implies that the *psi* waves are oscillatory in character. It is natural that some of our experiments, particularly those involving interference effects, are best described in terms of waves, although we realise these waves are merely a man-made device to calculate the results of such experiments. Others are best treated as the movements of particles, even though we know that these particles do not really exist between one collision and the next, and so do not actually *move*.

We have no difficulty accepting that these laws are non-causal in nature, for the familiar world of cause and effect at the macroscopic level can originate just as readily from a set of statistical rules in the microscopic world as it would if this world were itself ruled causally.

The Uncertainty Principle is not really a principle in its own right. There is no uncertainty concerning the times and places of *past* couplings, even though there may be uncertainty in our knowledge of them. However, we are unable to predict accurately the occurrence of *future* events because the past history of the world simply does not contain enough information to determine the future. We can make partial predictions, and the nature of these is encapsulated in the system of wave mechanics we have developed; the limitation of the information carried by the quantum wave function results in the Heisenberg Principle. One example is provided by the apparent impossibility of measuring simultaneously the position and speed of a particle. If we do not acknowledge the existence of a particle between one coupling and the next, however, the concept of its speed during that interval of time has vanished also. True, if we know the times and positions of two consecutive couplings we can divide the distance by the time and call the result 'speed', but this corresponds to no real property of the particle between these two times. On the other hand it does give us a value to put into our energy and momentum equations, and the relationship between pairs of consecutive *past* couplings is such that we find our conservation laws are satisfied. So what has now happened to the Heisenberg Principle? The time and position of a coupling are perfectly definite concepts, but until the next coupling has occurred, and we have a record of it, the speed of the particle between these two moments is no more than a fiction we invent to make predictions about that next coupling; as the predictions are necessarily incomplete, the speed we calculate must display the characteristic uncertainty.

Young's experiment is now easily understood, for the *psi* wave can instantaneously 'feel out' the layout of the whole apparatus; the *psi* values at the screen for the two possible routes must be added before squaring the modulus to find the probability distribution of the couplings that will occur there, so producing the observed light and dark bands. We now know it is meaningless to ask through which hole the particles pass, for they exist only at the source and at the screen, and not in between. Nor does the *psi* wave really pass through the holes, for *psi* is simply a representation of our knowledge. All that passes through the holes is the imaginary region where, if a coupling were to occur, it would be most likely. Moreover there is now no mystery about the effect of putting particle detectors close to the holes, for the experiment is then changed, with a new coupling occurring whenever a particle is detected. No longer do we add *psi* values for the two ways the particles can go, as the two routes now represent entirely different composite events; we must add the two *probabilities* instead of the *psi* values, and the interference pattern no longer exists. Feynman again is scornfully dismissive of those who argue otherwise. After stressing that in calculating the probability of an event it is essential to find a single final *psi* value to represent that whole event, even if it is composite, he writes,

> Keeping this principle in mind should help the student avoid being confused by things such as the 'reduction of the wave packet' and similar magic.

(*QED*, p.76, see Bibliography).

133

Many experiments have now been carried out, and many more suggested, in which a beam of photons or other particles is passed through two holes, or in some other way is split into two, producing an interference pattern on a screen, and then attempts are made to find out which of the two paths individual particles have followed. Invariably it is found that, when the path of each particle can be determined, the interference disappears. An alternative way to explain this phenomenon is in terms of the information that is carried by the (imaginary) wave form representing the trajectory of a particle; the *phase* of the wave is a part of this information, and it is this which determines, when there are two alternative paths, whether the two beams interfere constructively or destructively. Now any observation capable in principle of deciding which of the two paths has been followed, requires the siphoning off of this phase information, and so destroys the interference effect. A fascinating demonstration of this was described by M. S. Chapman *et al.* in 1995, and reported by T. Sudbery in *Nature* (Vol. 379, p. 403). A beam of atoms is split and recombined by using two diffraction gratings, and a laser beam shining across the apparatus illuminates the atoms as they move. If we suppose each atom scatters one photon, then that photon in theory contains enough information to determine which path the particular atom is following, and so the interference pattern vanishes. The experimenter could retrieve this information by focusing the photons with a lens, to form an image enabling him to determine which of the two paths the atom had traced. If, instead, he merely observed the *direction* in which each scattered photon was travelling, this would not be sufficient to decide which path the corresponding atom had followed, but the interference pattern would still be suppressed. It is not the act of observing which destroys interference, but the loss of phase information carried away by the scattered photons, whether or not anyone views them. This fact might seem obvious, but it has not always been made clear in the reporting of past experiments. One suspects authors have occasionally sought to sensationalise their results by suggesting that they are affected by the act of observing, whereas in fact they do not at all depend on whether anyone is actually watching the apparatus.

In the experiment at present under discussion, it is possible to store in a computer the position at which each atom strikes the screen, and the direction followed by the corresponding photon, and to study the results later at leisure. If the computer is then used to select all the photons which had been scattered in a particular direction, it is found that the corresponding atoms do, once again, show an interference pattern. At first sight this might seem astonishing; an observer is able to affect the results of an experiment *after it is completed*! But expressing the result in such a sensational way hides its real simplicity. By choosing only those photons which move in a certain direction the experimenter is putting information back into the system. The particular atoms corresponding to the selected photons have all been affected in the same way and so retain the phase differences which cause the interference; or viewing it differently, because the scattered photons all have the same direction they do not carry away information about which route the atoms have taken, and so the corresponding atoms can again form an interference pattern.

Viewed from this new position, Schrödinger's cat should no longer worry us. When a process starts at the quantum level there may be uncertainty over how far the quantum activity extends, but there can be no doubt that when a hammer smashes a flask of poison we are talking about a real happening. When describing the quantum world we must be careful to work with *psi* values rather than probabilities, because of the possibility of encountering quantum interference effects, but in the real world we can use either *psi* values or probabilities as we wish. If you choose to continue calculating the wave-function until the moment Schrödinger's box is opened, so be it, but I prefer to collapse my wave as soon as the nucleus has disintegrated. In any case there is no doubt that the dispersal of the poisonous fumes is an irreversible real event, and the unfortunate cat will die at once.

The EPR experiment is likewise explained without resorting to any extreme hypotheses. We know that a measurement performed on one particle may instantaneously affect the result of a measurement on the other, so long as no message can be sent between them. We must regret that Einstein lacked in later life that wonderful clarity of vision which produced the Theory of Relativity at the beginning of the century. Had he not started on the wrong foot in his discussions with Bohr, he was the one person who might have evaporated the mysteries of the quantum world in a way that would have convinced everyone, and saved a great deal of fruitless argument and much ink and paper.

Another phenomenon which led some experimenters to believe a physical system can be affected by our attempts to measure it is provided by the polarisation of light, and we now examine this using the new approach outlined above. Polaroid is a semi-transparent material, used in some sunglasses and photographic filters, possessing an 'axis of polarisation'. When unpolarised light falls on a sheet of polaroid it is found that one half of it is transmitted and the rest absorbed. When a second sheet is placed behind the first, then if the axes of the two filters are parallel, all the light passing through the first passes also through the second, but if the axes are at right-angles, none of the light passes through the second filter. For angles between zero and ninety degrees a simple formula tells us what proportion of the light passing through the first filter passes also through the second.

To explain this in terms of photons it must be supposed that each one has its own axis of polarisation, and the probability of a photon being transmitted through a polaroid filter depends upon the angle between its axis and that of the filter, as given by the same formula as that mentioned above. It should be clear, however, that this explanation is incomplete. When a stream of photons is beamed on two filters with their axes at right-angles, not all the photons passing through the first filter have their axes parallel to that of the filter; indeed the transmitted light would seem to contain photons at all angles, except for those exactly at right angles to this axis. It follows that a substantial (and calculable) proportion will then pass also through the second filter, which is not what we observe. The traditional explanation of this paradox maintains that passing the photons through the first filter is an act of *measurement*, whose effect on the photons which are transmitted is to change their axes so that they emerge exactly parallel to that of the filter. They will then all be blocked by the second filter. However, our new way of thinking makes this line of reasoning more plausible, for the photons which pass through the polaroid are just figments of our imagination. When a photon is *absorbed* by a sheet of polaroid, it undoubtedly engages in a coupling there, but if it is *transmitted*, there is no coupling. A photon which appears to pass through two such sheets has no real coupling at either; it cannot be said to exist between the point where it is generated and on the screen which finally detects its presence. It does not pass through the polarisers at all, although the wave form which describes the probabilities of its future behaviour must take into account their existence. The old wave theory of light had no difficulty explaining the action of the two filters, and the behaviour of the *psi* function is closely similar to that of the electromagnetic waves which were imagined in the nineteenth century. The only legitimate way of applying quantum mechanics to the problem is to use *psi* values to predict the probabilities of a photon being stopped by each of the filters or by the screen placed behind them; only this imaginary waveform is changed by its passage through the first filter.

CONCLUSIONS

So the philosophical conclusions we reach from a study of this branch of science are profound, but not quite as disturbing as is suggested by some writers. Perhaps the most important is the denial that the influence of particles on one another is local. The presence of a particle or the layout of an experiment is 'known' everywhere in the universe, and because of relativity's denial of simultaneity, at times both before and after the present. This is not something we can be aware of directly, for the influence can act only by changing the probabilities of distant quantum events, and impinges only indirectly on the real world of our experience.

The discovery of a random element in the activity of the quantum world must also be cause for much thought, but again it has little effect on the everyday world, for so great is the number of quantum events involved in any activity we can observe directly that the statistical laws of the atomic world become strict deterministic laws at our own level of experience. Eddington provided a telling analogy:

Human life is proverbially uncertain; few things are more certain than the solvency of a life-insurance company.

The 'hidden variable' question remains open. Einstein believed that eventually we would find the quantum world to be deterministic, with hidden laws enabling us to predict its behaviour from one moment to the next in the same way that we could predict the spin of a coin if we knew everything about its motion. There seems no way of disproving this theory, but the EPR experiments make it less likely, for the non-local nature of the wave-form laws would remain even if the theory were true. It seems simpler to suppose that quantum phenomena are random, only their probabilities being connected by universal laws.

The reality of the material world has survived our scrutiny, although it is perhaps less substantial than some might have hoped. The particles of which the world is composed are real enough, but only at the moments when they interact with each other. We can know nothing about them in between these interactions, and it seems best to deny the reality of the trajectories which we can draw and visualise so glibly.

What we have attempted to show in this chapter is the irrelevance of *consciousness* to the behaviour of the quantum world. The *psi* waves we use to define probabilities, and which evolve with the passage of time, are the product of our intelligence, and closely related to the imperfect knowledge we have as a result of memories and records being necessarily of the past. However, the underlying rules relating the real couplings of which the world consists owe nothing to consciousness. They are time-symmetric, whereas everything relating to human consciousness is heavily tainted with the asymmetry provided by memory and the illusory passage of time from past to future. An act of measuremant or observation certainly changes the wave function we have constructed, but has no effect on the real world of particle couplings. The Universe existed long before the first conscious beings began to observe it, and will continue long after the last one perishes.

Chapter 9

CONCLUSIONS

PHILOSOPHICAL THOUGHT

We began by asking why several important but apparently simple questions, concerning the world in general and our place within it, are still unresolved after centuries of thinking, debating and writing. What is it about these philosophical problems, or what is it about the way they have been approached, that makes them so refractory?

During much of this period, of course, scientific knowledge and understanding were very unreliable. When we consider how inaccurate was the teaching of the chemists, biologists and astronomers of past centuries perhaps we should not be surprised that beliefs concerning less specific matters were also in dispute, for they had to be based either on facts that were themselves false or doubtful, or on the equally unsafe foundation of introspection. Today our factual knowledge is much more complete, and covers areas which previous generations had considered unsuitable for the precise and logical methods of science, yet some of the fundamental problems of philosophy remain as controversial as ever.

This book has attempted to show that our thinking is sometimes circumscribed by other difficulties which are not so inevitable as scientific ignorance, and which increasing knowledge is doing little to dissipate. One of these is the inflated opinion we hold of our own importance. There is still a tendency to assume implicitly that mankind is more important than anything else in the Universe. We devote so much energy to resolving human problems and so little to pondering questions of wider significance that we have difficulty approaching these in terms other than human ones. We believe unthinkingly that the Universe exists to provide us with a home, and that its meaning can be discovered by studying ourselves. Our lives are so dominated by questions of motive and intention, of language and argument, of right and wrong, that we can barely contemplate an outside world in which these concepts have no meaning. Chapter Two was an attempt to show how insignificant is mankind's place in the Universe as a whole; we have no right to project onto it the methods and values which we have developed to cope with our own little world.

Another difficulty standing in the way of clear thought is our false impression of the nature of time. Chapter Three maintained that our belief in a 'now', which continually moves, and which divides a region of certainty which we call 'the past' from one whose contents are still uncertain called 'the future', is an illusion, arising only because we have brains which can store memories of the past but not the future. In possessing this faculty we are certainly untypical and may possibly be unique; there might be no structures anywhere in the universe apart from the brains of living beings on earth (and some of man's own inventions, such as books, video cameras and computers) where accurate records exist of past events; and in the absence of creatures with memories there is no such thing as 'now'. To avoid the pitfalls which our distorted view presents in the search for truth we must often employ the picture developed in Chapter Four of a four-dimensional world, with three dimensions of space and one of time, whereby we can visualise the history of a system as a static display without any suggestion of change.

A NEW APPROACH

Trying to avoid these two obstacles, we looked firstly at the question of causation, which we found to be a natural consequence of the precise physical laws governing events and their relationships, laws which are best visualised as constraints on the linkages between points on our four-dimensional model. The apparent time asymmetry of cause and effect was seen to arise only because of our own prejudiced viewpoint, and our belief in the uncertainty of the future.

We next tried to apply these principles to a discussion of free will. Explaining clearly what we mean by free will proved difficult; some people's definitions we found to be almost meaningless. If confronted with the assertion that intelligent beings have a non-physical component, a 'mind', which can over-ride the normal laws of cause and effect in the brain then we maintained that, while this suggestion cannot be disproved at the present time, it does nothing to advance the argument concerning free will. We did accept, however, the rather vague claim of most people that they can control their own actions; the decision-making process may be wholly deterministic, but it is so complex and often involves such conflict that we are deceived into feeling it must transcend the rigid laws of science.

Chapter Six was devoted to human behaviour, and in particular to the meaning of right and wrong, good and evil. We found these concepts closely related to the needs of human civilisation; behaviour is often demanded which conflicts with inherited tendencies, for these have not changed rapidly enough to keep pace with the requirements of living in a society. Communities have discovered how to foster altruistic behaviour by teaching us to admire it when we see it in others. We also considered the mystery of human consciousness; once again this may make us and some animals unique in the whole of creation. It was not found helpful to seek an explanation lying beyond the scope of normal scientific investigation; the sheer complexity of our mental processes can explain why we become aware of them.

PURPOSE

We asked in Chapter Two whether the universe was unfolding in pursuit of some purpose, or whether its whole history, including the development of life, was a random process, driven only by the laws of nature and the rules of *chance*. Are we now in a better position to answer this question?

To avoid the risk of a purely verbal argument let us agree on a meaning for the word *purpose*. We certainly recognise purpose in much human activity; a young person attends college or university with the purpose of gaining knowledge for his future work and hobbies; he applies for a job with the purpose of earning a living, buys a house to have somewhere comfortable to live and marries so that he can raise a family. In each of these cases a number of alternatives present themselves and he uses his knowledge and powers of reasoning to predict the likely outcome of each alternative, finally making a decision which, if he has a strong 'sense of purpose', is determined more by the probability of long-term advantage than the satisfaction of immediate wishes. The essential feature of purposeful activity is an ability to predict the likely results of different courses of action, and to use the results of these predictions in determining the course to be followed.

So is purpose purely a feature of human thinking? Behaviour which is apparently purposeful is often observed in the animal kingdom. The sight of a bird building its nest can prove an object lesson to someone whose own decisions are too often determined by short-term gain or satisfaction. Can we say that the bird is motivated by purpose? A definite answer cannot be given, for it depends on the creature's state of mind. If it has a mental picture of the finished nest and of the family it hopes to rear there at a later time, together with a realisation that failure to attend to the task will lead to homelessness later, then the bird certainly has a sense of purpose. This is not so if it merely acts out a role which nature has programmed for it, without an image of the outcome of its work. The essence of purpose is an intelligent being's visualisation of the future consequences of a contemplated action, and the striving to achieve those consequences in the face of conflicting urges. In this way purpose becomes one of the factors entering the decision-making process, and indeed is the one factor which contributes most to our belief in the freedom of the will. Purpose can have significance only for creatures with sufficient intellect to predict possible outcomes of present behaviour, but without the omniscience to know for certain in advance that a particular outcome will actually occur. Like several other questions we have discussed, whether or not the Universe has a purpose proves very difficult to define meaningfully.

CHANCE

Are we driven to conclude that the direction in which the world evolves is determined purely by chance? We certainly see the hand of chance at work as we watch the movements of the galaxies, the stars and the planets. In 1994 a comet struck the planet Jupiter with a force equivalent to a million million tons of explosive. If it had been the earth rather than Jupiter the resulting debris would have polluted our atmosphere so severely that all life could have been extinguished. Indeed it is thought likely that such a collision did occur some 65 million years ago, destroying much of the life that covered the earth at that time, including all the species of dinosaur.

We see chance at work equally today as we observe the lives of our fellow men and women. It would be good to think that the most worthy and honourable of our colleagues are the ones who enjoy good fortune, but we know otherwise. Many of the misfortunes and disasters which overtake individuals and communities are the result of pure chance.

Chance also appears to have played a large part in the evolution of life here. The *direction* of evolution has been guided by the simple process of 'survival of the fittest', but the *driving force* has been the random mutations which enable creatures, quite by accident, to produce offspring with different characteristics from their own. For every creature born with an advantage over its peers many more must have appeared with grotesque deformities ensuring they could not survive. The process is random, but it is easy to understand how it has resulted in ever more complex and successful beings. Once the first molecules had appeared which could reproduce themselves and draw nourishment from their environment, the evolution of ever higher life forms was an inevitable consequence of the process of mutation and selection.

One great mystery remains. We are as yet unable to

manufacture artificially a single molecule sufficiently complicated to reproduce itself, and so to become the starting point from which life can develop, nor do we know how easy or difficult it would prove to produce such a molecule. Many experts believe that, as the earth cooled down and water began to collect in the hollows, conditions would allow such molecules to form. The 'primordial soup' would contain a rich solution of many substances including all the elements necessary for life; if a high energy source were needed then this would sometimes be provided by flashes of lightning.

It is often forgotten that, however improbable may be the formation of living molecules from inanimate matter, if there is the remotest chance of it happening anywhere in the universe, then the problem of our existence is solved. Let us consider some figures. The total number of stars is about ten thousand million million million. Many astronomers believe that most will have a set of planets in orbit around them, but if we suppose that only one star in a thousand possesses such a system, and that in each system only one planet is suitable for life, then we still have ten million million million such planets. Now suppose the probability of a living molecule forming on any given planet is one in a million. Most people would regard this as a very small likelihood; you are much more likely to be killed by lightning! Yet the number of planets on which life has appeared, or will appear, would then be no less than ten million million. If life fails to take a hold in nine hundred and ninety nine out of every one thousand planets on which a living molecule forms, and if *intelligent* life develops on only one in a thousand of those on which it *does* take hold, then we still have ten million planets on which intelligent life develops.

Suppose now the probability of living molecules forming on a given planet is not one in a million, but only one in a million million. This is very close to impossibility; if two people each decide independently to hide a coin somewhere in Great Britain, the probability that the two coins will be within *twelve inches* of each other is about one in a million million. And yet if the emergence of a living molecule on a given planet has this tiny likelihood, and we make the same assumptions as in the previous paragraph, there will still be about ten planets on which intelligent life develops. So if we maintain that life arises purely by chance, it matters not that the probability of such an event may be infinitesimally small.

RELIGIOUS BELIEF

Before ending this brief investigation into some of the world's most intriguing problems, we must ask whether our philosophy is compatible with any rationally held religious beliefs. Can a God exist alongside the universe we have described, and if so what function would He fulfil and how must our picture of the world be modified to accommodate His influence?

Simply discussing the existence of God is usually a fruitless exercise, for most of us are able to give a definition of God which satisfies our own beliefs. Many who claim to be believers have themselves created the God in whom they believe. Only the relationship of God to the material world and to mankind can promote valuable discussion.

Can we believe in a deity who plays an active part in the world we inhabit by reacting with the material bodies it contains? If there is no universal 'now' there appears to be no point of contact at which such action can occur; the only way God could affect the running of the world, in the sense that its history will differ from what it would be without Him, must be by influencing the space-time causal network so that the rules of science are broken at some points, and there is little evidence of this ever happening. If the children of Israel did indeed pass through the Red Sea, with a wall of water 'on their right hand, and on their left' (Exodus, 14), then the laws of physics must have been infringed, with irregular forces moving the water from its normal configuration, and the rules of gravitation being suspended until Moses stretched forth his hand over the sea, and Pharoah's troops were engulfed. We can understand how the superstitious people of the day, with no knowledge of the laws of nature, could believe such a story, but today most will hesitate to take it literally, believing rather that the facts must have become distorted, perhaps by reason of repeated telling and re-telling before it was written down. Our present viewpoint, with its insistence that wrong

145

conceptions of time can invalidate much of our thinking, renders such stories even less plausible. The idea of a God, so appalled at the plight of the Israelites that He takes the extreme action of suspending the laws of Nature to avoid a catastrophe He had not foreseen, presupposes that God suffers from the same blinkered view of history as we ourselves, a view imposed on us by our physical brains, constrained by the principles of Thermodynamics. Miracles are better explained by human misunderstanding than by divine intervention.

There remains the possibility that God, while not reacting directly with the material world, may be able to influence the minds of men and women, and achieve His purpose by intervening in the decision-making process. There are many examples of people whose beliefs have suffered a sudden conversion, or who have decided on the spur of the moment to devote the rest of their lives to serving good causes; in some cases an immediate reason can be identified, such as a harrowing experience or a moving sermon, while others may be attributed by some observers to divine influence. But the argument we advanced in Chapter Five, that our actions must either be caused deterministically or random, still applies. If indeed God can play a part in deciding our actions, the outer box we drew around Fig. 9 must now enclose God Himself, and His intervention becomes part of the causal chain determining our actions; it becomes an element in decision-making on equal terms with any other aspect of our nature or our character. We all know people whose behaviour can often be described as godly or saintly, but this shows only that these people's nature incorporates elements of godliness; no active intervention from outside in the making of individual decisions is required, and nor is it possible within the framework we are describing. What certainly *can* influence the way we behave is the ethical training we receive in childhood, training which may well be underpinned by a religious framework and the example of godly people whom we try to emulate throughout life, whether consciously or otherwise.

Philosophers and theologians have long argued over whether God has knowledge of future events as well as of the past. If He has, then the future must in some sense already be determined, and man's apparent capacity to change the future by the exercise of his will, a capacity at the heart of most systems of religious ethics, must be illusory. If He has not, then God can no longer be considered omniscient; indeed His thinking must be circumscribed by a limitation which, as we have seen, is imposed on human thought only because of man's material limitations. As the Roman philosopher Boethius wrote nearly fifteen hundred years ago,

> If God beholdeth all things and cannot be deceived, then what He foreseeth must inevitably happen. Wherefore if from eternity He doth foreknow not only the deeds of men but also their counsels and their will, there can be no free will.

But we can now see that the problem presents a deeper contradiction than this, for what can possibly be meant by a non-physical God having *any* sort of knowledge? When we talk of man having knowledge of some (past) event, we are referring to the memory of that event which exists within his brain; a structural arrangement of his nerve-cells represents the details of the event according to a pre-arranged code. Nowhere else in the material universe is there evidence of one thing representing another in this way except in the brains of intelligent creatures on earth and in man's record-keeping inventions. It is meaningless to talk of knowledge existing in the absence of a substantial medium such as brain-cells, paper, or magnetic coatings, onto which that knowledge can be written. To assert that God has knowledge, whether of the past or the future, is to distort the meaning of that word beyond recognition; once again we find a philosophical argument which has proved sterile not because it has been pursued at insufficient depth, but because its meaning vanishes when scrutinised.

Many who deny that God is at work in the world today, nevertheless attribute the original act of Creation to divine agency. We must not visualise Him existing in time before the big bang, and actually initiating the explosion, for time itself did not exist before the creation. But several cosmologists have drawn attention in recent years to the fact that the fundamental constants of nature, such as the mass and charge of the electron and proton, the constant of gravitation, and the speed of light, appear to be fine-tuned to make possible the emergence of life. Even a tiny change in any of these constants could have resulted in a world

147

with entirely different properties from ours, in which life as we know it would have been impossible. Perhaps the lifetime of the Universe would then have been too short for life to develop, or life's essential elements might never have been formed, or the nuclear reaction which powers the sun and stars might have been impossible. Indeed, so critically dependent is our universe on these constants of nature that some scientists are driven to conclude it must have been *designed* to harbour life, and they attribute this to divine agency. If we believe this, have not our thinkers been in a similar position many times before, only to discover subsequently that what seemed the result of careful planning is just the working out of simple natural laws, rather than evidence of a non-physical influence? Before the nature of the earth and the sun were understood, man attributed to the gods the sunshine, the rain and the fertility of the soil on which his crops depended. Later, when these phenomena were understood, the existence on earth of just those chemical elements needed for the formation of living beings was again thought to be evidence of marvellous design. Later still, the complexity of the human body and brain could only be explained as the work of a benign Creator. Now that we can explain the suitability of the earth for living creatures by recalling the Anthropic Principle, the existence of the chemical elements by quoting the Quantum Theory, and the development of human life by the process of evolution, we no longer invoke God to account for them. Is it not likely that, in just the same way, values of the constants of nature will someday be fully understood, with science showing them to be calculable and inevitable, and not the result of careful design? Shall we not then have to accept our existence as remarkable good fortune? The strength of this argument, that the values of nature's constants were chosen for our benefit, is further reduced by our inability to work out in detail the type of universe that would have resulted if the values *had* been different. We have no idea whether such values could have allowed the development of an entirely different form of life, or of some even more exotic phenomena which we cannot imagine. If intelligent beings *had* appeared in such a universe, would they not have believed, as we seem tempted to do, that the fundamental constants had been carefully chosen to make *them* possible?

Even if such beings would indeed be impossible in a universe with different characteristics to ours, can we not appeal once again to the Anthropic Principle to account for our existence? When we explain the remarkable suitability of the earth in this way, we rely on tther being millions of planets elsewhere with widely differing conditions; if the earth is the most suitable of them all, the Anthropic Principle teaches us that we did not choose *it*; rather the opposite is true, in that its very suitability explains why we are here, and not elsewhere. Is it possible that many other Universes may exist, each with its own values for the constants of nature? The Anthropic Principle would then explain why we exist in *this* one, with its apparently carefully designed properties to make us possible. We observe such an ideal universe because life will never form in those which are less suitable. Once again we need not seek a supernatural explanation of our good fortune.

However, science alone has no explanation for the secret of existence. Perhaps someday we shall discover that, if a universe is to exist, it must have the properties we observe in this one; but whether or not this comes about, how can we rule out the other alternative, just nothingness, the total absence of anything? If we wish to invoke the existence of God to explain why anything exists at all, it seems unlikely that science will ever displace Him from this role. Here at least is a God in whom everyone should be able to believe. What we do deny is that the existence of the Universe shows God to have a *purpose*, since purpose is a meaningless concept for a being without a physical brain like ours, a memory restricted by the laws of Thermodynamics to the past only, and a false belief in 'the present' and a moving time.

Most will agree that, on balance, the effects of religious belief on civilisation have been beneficial, despite the atrocities that have been committed in the name of religion, and the periods of history it has blighted. Among the ranks of the great, some have been inspired by their faith to live lives of noble self-sacrifice for the good of their fellows, and some have produced magnificent works of art, architecture and music which bring delight to millions. Many others have been helped to live upright lives by a belief that the canons of good behaviour are divine, and so deserve closer adherence than any man-made laws. Many derive comfort and support amid the disappointments and tragedies of earthly life from the belief in a happier world awaiting them after death. We can easily understand why those who profess religious belief wish to promulgate their doctrine as widely as possible; those who do not share their faith have no right to discourage this, and whether they call themselves atheists, agnostics or humanists they serve no useful purpose in attempting to convert others to their doctrine.

The many different faiths evident at the present time and throughout history make it difficult for any group to claim that theirs is 'true' and the others false, but the universality of some such faith in almost every primitive community suggests that man has a natural tendency to believe in the supernatural. Such belief makes little contact with mainstream scientific research, but will probably always play a part in many people's thinking.

CONCLUSION

Stated in its baldest terms, then, life on earth appears to be just a chemical reaction which occurred in a hot swamp four billion years ago and got out of control, but there is no reason to feel depressed or discouraged by this philosophy; indeed it can be seen as challenging and stimulating. Our own lives, those of our descendants, and the very future of life itself, depend upon our own decisions and our own efforts. There is no source of advice, natural or supernatural, to which we can turn if we make a mess of our own lives or of the planet on which they depend. It is up to each one of us to take the fullest possible advantage of the wonderful bodies and brains with which the random process of evolution has endowed us, and which we did nothing to deserve. Each of us lives only one life, during which we can contribute, in whatever ways our particular talents allow, to the world about us and to the lives of our fellow men and women. The idea of a purpose behind the cosmos as a whole may be without meaning, but the concept of purpose is certainly meaningful in relation to our own behaviour. If nature does not provide us with one then we must each provide our own, and strive during our own few years to achieve the aims we set ourselves. One of the greatest contributions we can make to the life of our society is to bring children into the world, and equip them to take their place in the community and live valuable and fulfilling lives. Some people are able to contribute in other ways, by creating works of art or scholarship great enough to survive them, and in small ways we can all add something to the lives of those with whom we make daily contact, and try to leave the world a little better than we found it.

Our complex and rich civilisation has arisen and flourished only because of the dedication and vision of men and women throughout the ages, and it is by the endeavours of our own and future generations that we will continue to grow in understanding of the natural world, to share more advantageously the limited resources of the planet, and to explore ever more widely the opportunities offered by the amazing gift of life which chance has bestowed upon us.

THE END

BIBLIOGRAPHY

Atkins, P.W., *The Second Law*, Scientific American Books (1984).

Blackburn, S., *The Oxford Dictionary of Philosophy,* OUP (1994).

Brody, T., *The Philosophy behind Physics*, Springer-Verlag (1993).

Coveney, P. and Highfield, R., *The Arrow of Time*, Allen (1990).

Davies, P.C.W., *Space and Time in the Modern Universe*, CUP (1977).

Davies, P.C.W. and Brown, J.R. (ed.), *The Ghost in the Atom*, CUP (1986).

Davies, P.C.W., *About Time*, Viking (1995).

Davies, P.C.W and Betts, D.S., *Quantum Mechanics*, Chapman & Hall (1994).

Eddington, A.S., *The Nature of the Physical World*, CUP (1928).

Einstein, A. (translated by Lawson, R.W.), *Relativity*, Methuen (1920).

Feynman, R., *The Character of Physical Law*, M.I.T. (1965).

Feynman, R.P., *Q.E.D.*, Penguin (1985).

French, A.P. and Taylor, E.F., *Introduction to Quantum Physics*, Chapman & Hall (1979).

Gribbin, J., *In Search of Schrödinger's Cat*, Corgi (1984).

Gribbin, J., *In the Beginning*, BCA (1993).

Hawking, S.W., *A Brief History of Time*, Guild Publishing (1988).

Hollis, M., *Invitation to Philosophy*, Blackwell (1985).

Isaacs, A. (ed.), *A Concise Dictionary of Physics,* OUP (1990).

Magee, B., *Men of Ideas*, OUP (1978).

Penrose, R., *The Emperor's New Mind*, OUP (1989).

Polkinghorne, J.C., *The Quantum World*, Penguin (1984).

Russell, B., *The Problems of Philosophy*, OUP (1912).

Russell, B., *History of Western Philosophy,* Routledge (1946).

Watson, G.(ed), *Free Will*, OUP (1982).

Zohar, D., *The Quantum Self*, Flamingo (1991).

INDEX

156

158